Henry Edward Manning

The Vatican Decrees in Their Bearing on Civil Allegiance

Henry Edward Manning

The Vatican Decrees in Their Bearing on Civil Allegiance

ISBN/EAN: 9783337424787

Printed in Europe, USA, Canada, Australia, Japan

Cover: Foto ©Lupo / pixelio.de

More available books at **www.hansebooks.com**

THE
VATICAN DECREES

IN THEIR BEARING ON

CIVIL ALLEGIANCE.

BY

HENRY EDWARD,

ARCHBISHOP OF WESTMINSTER.

NEW YORK:
THE CATHOLIC PUBLICATION SOCIETY,
9 WARREN STREET.

1875.

CONTENTS.

	PAGE
INTRODUCTION,	7

CHAPTER.
- I. MEANING AND EFFECT OF THE VATICAN DECREES, ... 17
- II. THE RELATIONS OF THE SPIRITUAL AND CIVIL POWERS, ... 46
- III. AGGRESSIONS OF THE CIVIL POWER, . . . 94
- IV. TRUE AND FALSE PROGRESS, . . . 123
- V. THE MOTIVE OF THE DEFINITION, . . . 148

CONCLUSION, ... 166

APPENDICES, ... 171

PREFACE.

A TASK both difficult and unlooked for has suddenly fallen to my lot; that is, to gain a fair hearing on subjects about which the opinions, and still more the feelings, of so many men are not only adverse, but even hostile. I must, therefore, ask for patience from those who may read these pages.

The topics here treated have not been chosen by me. They have been raised by Mr. GLADSTONE, and perhaps, in all the range of Religion and Politics, none can be found more delicate, more beset with misconceptions, or more prejudged by old traditionary beliefs and antipathies. Some of them, too, are of an odious kind; others revive memories we would fain forget. And yet, if Mr. GLADSTONE'S appeal to me is to be answered, treated they must be. My reply to the argument of the Expostulation on the Vatican Council will be found in the first, second, and fifth chapters; but as Mr. GLADSTONE has brought into his impeachment the present conflict in Germany, and has reviewed his own conduct in respect to the Revolution in Italy, I have felt myself obliged to follow him. This I have done in the third and fourth chapters. Apart from this reason, I felt myself bound to do so by the terms of the two letters printed at the opening of the following pages. I hold myself pledged to justify their contents. Moreover, these two topics fall within the outline of the subject treated by Mr. GLADSTONE, which is, the relation of the Supreme Spiritual Power of the Head of the Christian Church to the Civil Powers of all countries. So much for the matter of these pages.

As for the manner, if it be faulty, the fault is mine: and yet there ought to be no fault imputed where there has been no intention to wound or to offend. I can say with truth that, to avoid offence, I have weighed my words, and if there be one still found which ought not to have been written, I wish it to be blotted out. The subject-matter is beyond my control. I can blot out words, but I cannot blot out truths. What I believe to be truth, that I have said in the clearest words and calmest that I could find to give to it adequate expression.

THE VATICAN DECREES

IN THEIR BEARING ON

CIVIL ALLEGIANCE.

INTRODUCTION.

Mr. Gladstone, in his Expostulation with the Catholics of the British Empire on the Decrees of the Vatican Council, writes as follows:—

'England is entitled to ask and to know in what way the obedience required by the Pope and the Council of the Vatican is to be reconciled with the integrity of Civil Allegiance.'[1]

When I read these words, I at once recognized the right of the English people, speaking by its legitimate authorities, to know from me what I believe and what I teach; but in recognising this right I am compelled to decline to answer before any other tribunal, or to any other interrogator. If, therefore, I take the occasion of any such interrogation, I do not address myself to those who make it, but to the justice and to the good sense of the Christian people of this country.

[1] *The Vatican Decrees in their Bearing on Civil Allegiance.* By the Right Hon. W. E. Gladstone. P. 43.

Mr. Gladstone followed up this demand upon his Catholic fellow-countrymen by an elaborate argument to prove that it is impossible for Catholics, since the Vatican Council, to be loyal except at the cost of their fidelity to the Council, or faithful to the Council except at the cost of their loyalty to their country. I therefore considered it to be my duty to lose no time in making the subjoined declaration in all our principal journals.

'SIR,—The gravity of the subject on which I address you, affecting, as it must, every Catholic in the British Empire, will, I hope, obtain from your courtesy the publication of this letter.

'This morning I received a copy of a pamphlet, entitled "The Vatican Decrees in their Bearing on Civil Allegiance." I find in it a direct appeal to myself, both for the office I hold and for the writings I have published. I gladly acknowledge the duty that lies upon me for both those reasons. I am bound by the office I bear not to suffer a day to pass without repelling from the Catholics of this country the lightest imputation upon their loyalty; and, for my teaching, I am ready to show that the principles I have ever taught are beyond impeachment upon that score.

'It is true, indeed, that in page 57 of the pamphlet Mr. Gladstone expresses his belief "that many of his Roman Catholic friends and fellow-countrymen are, to say the least of it, as good citizens as himself." But as the whole pamphlet is an elaborate argument to prove that the teaching of the Vatican Council renders it impossible for them to be so, I cannot accept this grateful acknowledgment, which implies that they are good citizens because they are at variance with the Catholic Church.

'I should be wanting in duty to the Catholics of this country and to myself if I did not give a prompt contradiction to this statement, and if I did not with equal promptness affirm that the loyalty of our civil allegiance is, not in spite of the teaching of the Catholic Church, but because of it.

'The sum of the argument in the pamphlet just published to the world is this:—That by the Vatican Decrees such a change has been made in the relations of Catholics to the civil power of States, that it is no longer possible for them to render the same undivided civil allegiance as it was possible for Catholics to render before the promulgation of those Decrees.

'In answer to this it is for the present sufficient to affirm—

'1. That the Vatican Decrees have in no jot or tittle changed either the obligations or the conditions of civil allegiance.

'2. That the civil allegiance of Catholics is as undivided as that of all Christians, and of all men who recognise a Divine or natural moral law.

'3. That the civil allegiance of no man is unlimited; and therefore the civil allegiance of all men who believe in God, or are governed by conscience, is in that sense divided.

'4. In this sense, and in no other, can it be said with truth that the civil allegiance of Catholics is divided. The civil allegiance of every Christian man in England is limited by conscience and the law of God; and the civil allegiance of Catholics is limited neither less nor more.

'5. The public peace of the British Empire has been consolidated in the last half century by the elimination of religious conflicts and inequalities from our laws. The Empire of Germany might have been equally peaceful and stable if its statesmen had not been tempted in an evil hour to rake up the old fires of religious disunion. The hand of one man, more than any other, threw this torch of discord into the German Empire. The history of Germany will record the name of Dr. Ignatius von Döllinger as the author of this national evil. I lament, not only to read the name, but to trace the arguments of Dr. von Döllinger in the pamphlet before me. May God preserve these kingdoms from the public and private calamities which are visibly impending over Germany. The author of the pamphlet, in his first line, assures us that his "purpose is not polemical but pacific." I am sorry that so good an intention should have so widely erred in the selection of the means.

'But my purpose is neither to criticise nor to controvert. My desire and my duty as an Englishman, as a Catholic, and as a pastor, is to claim for my flock and for myself a civil allegiance as pure, as true, and as loyal as is rendered by the distinguished author of the pamphlet, or by any subject of the British Empire.

&c. &c.

'*November* 7, 1874.'

Subsequently, in reply to questions proposed to me, I further wrote as follows:—

To the Editor of *The New York Herald.*

'Dear Sir,—In answer to your question as to my statement about the Vatican Council, I reply as follows:

'I asserted that the Vatican Decrees have not changed by a jot or a tittle the obligations or conditions of the civil obedience of Catholics towards the Civil Powers. The whole of Mr. Gladstone's pamphlet hangs on the contrary assertion; and falls with it. In proof of my assertion I add:—

'1. That the Infallibility of the Pope was a doctrine of Divine Faith before the Vatican Council was held. In the second and third parts of a book called "Petri Privilegium (Longmans, 1871), I have given more than sufficient evidence of this assertion.

'2. That the Vatican Council simply declared an old truth, and made no new dogma.

'3. That the position of Catholics therefore in respect to civil allegiance, since the Vatican Council, is precisely what it was before it.

'4. That the Civil Powers of the Christian world have hitherto stood in peaceful relation with an Infallible Church, and that relation has been often recognised and declared by the Church in its Councils. The Vatican Council had, therefore, no new matter to treat in this point.

'5. That the Vatican Council has made no decree whatever on the subject of the Civil Powers, nor on civil allegiance.

'This subject was not so much as proposed. The civil obedience of Catholics rests upon the natural law, and the revealed law of God. Society is founded in nature, and subjects are bound in all things lawful to obey their rulers. Society, when Christian, has higher sanctions, and subjects are bound to obey rulers for conscience sake, and because the Powers that be are ordained of God. Of all these things the Vatican Decrees can have changed nothing because they have touched nothing. Mr. Gladstone's whole argument hangs upon an erroneous assertion, into which I can only suppose he has been misled by his misplaced trust in Dr. Döllinger and some of his friends.

'On public and private grounds I deeply lament this act of imprudence, and but for my belief in Mr. Gladstone's sincerity I should say this act of injustice. I lament it, as an act out of all harmony and proportion to a great statesman's life, and as the first event that has overcast a friendship of forty-five years. His whole public life has hitherto consolidated the Christian and civil peace of these kingdoms. This act, unless the good providence of God and the good sense of Englishmen avert it, may wreck more than the work of Mr. Gladstone's public career, and at the end of a long life may tarnish a great name

&c. &c.

'*Westminster, Nov.* 10, 1874.'

Having thus directly contradicted the main error of Mr. Gladstone's argument, I thought it my duty to wait. I was certain that two things would follow: the one, that far better answers than any that I could make would be promptly made; the other, that certain nominal Catholics, who upon other occasions have done the same, would write letters to the newspapers.

Both events have come to pass.

The Bishops of Birmingham, Clifton, and Salford have abundantly pointed out the mistakes into which Mr. Gladstone has fallen on the subject of the Vatican Council; and have fully vindicated the loyalty of Catholics.

The handful of nominal Catholics have done their work; and those who hoped to find or to make a division among Catholics have been disappointed. It is now seen that those who reject the Vatican Council may be told on our fingers, and the Catholic Church has openly passed sentence on them.

Having made these declarations, I might have remained silent; but as in my first letter I implied that I was prepared to justify what I had asserted, I gave notice that I would do so. Having passed my word, I will keep it; and in keeping it I will endeavour to deserve again the acknowledgment Mr. Gladstone has already made. He says that, whatever comes, so far as I am concerned, it will not be 'without due notice.' I will be equally outspoken now; not because he has challenged it, but because, so far as I know, I have always tried to speak out. In all these years of strife I have never consciously kept back, or explained away, any doctrine of the Catholic Church. I will not begin to do so now, when my time is nearly run. I am afraid that in these pages I shall seem to obtrude myself too often, and too much. If any think so, I would ask them to remember that Mr. Gladstone has laid me under this necessity in these three ways:—

1. He has made me the representative of the Catholic doctrine since 1870, as Bishop Doyle, he says, was in better days.
2. He has quoted my writings four times in censure.
3. He has appealed to me as 'Head of the Papal Church in England;' I may also add as 'The Oracle.' My words, however, shall not be ambiguous.

The two letters given above contain four assertions.

First, that the Decrees of the Vatican Council have changed nothing in respect to the civil obedience of Catholics.

Secondly, that their civil obedience is neither more nor less divided than that of other men.

Thirdly, that the relations of the Spiritual and Civil Powers have been fixed from time immemorial, and are therefore after the Vatican Council what they were before.

Fourthly, that the contest now waging abroad began in a malevolent and mischievous intrigue to instigate the Civil Powers to oppress and persecute the Catholic Church.

The two first propositions shall be treated in the first chapter, the third in the second chapter, and the last in the third.

I will therefore endeavour to prove the following propositions, which cover all the assertions I have made :—

1. That the Vatican Decrees have in no jot or tittle changed either the obligations or the conditions of Civil Allegiance.

2. That the relations of the Catholic Church to the Civil Powers of the world have been immutably fixed from the beginning, inasmuch as they arise out of the Divine Constitution of the Church, and out of the Civil Society of the natural order.

3. That any collisions now existing have been brought on by changes, not on the part of the Catholic Church, much less of the Vatican Council, but on the part of the Civil Powers, and that by reason of a systematic conspiracy against the Holy See.

4. That by these changes and collisions the Civil Powers of Europe are destroying their own stability.

5. That the motive of the Vatican Council in defining the Infallibility of the Roman Pontiff was not any temporal policy, nor was it for any temporal end; but that it defined that

truth in the face of all temporal dangers, in order to guard the Divine deposit of Christianity, and to vindicate the divine certainty of faith.

CHAPTER I.

MEANING AND EFFECT OF THE VATICAN DECREES.

I. IN setting out to prove my first proposition—namely, 'that the Vatican Decrees have in no jot or tittle changed either the obligations or the conditions of Civil Allegiance'—I find myself undertaking to prove a negative. The *onus* of proving that the Vatican Decrees have made a change in our civil allegiance rests upon those who affirm it. Till they offer proof we might remain silent. It would be enough for us to answer that the Vatican Council in its Dogmatic Constitution on the Church has simply affirmed the revealed doctrine of the Spiritual Primacy, and of the Infallibility of the Visible Head of the Christian Church; that the relations of this Primacy to the Civil Powers are in no way treated; and that the civil obedience of subjects is left precisely as and where it was before the Vatican Council was convened.

(1) However, I will first examine what proofs have been offered to show that the Vatican Council has made the alleged change; and I will then give positive evidence to show what the Vatican Council has done. From these things it will be seen that it has neither changed, nor added to, nor taken away anything from the doctrine and discipline of the Church, but has only defined what has been believed and practised from the beginning.

The arguments to prove a change are two.

First. Mr. Gladstone has argued from the third chapter of the Constitution on the Roman Pontiff, that his powers have received a great extension. Mr. Gladstone, so far as I am aware, is the first and only person who has ever ventured on this statement.

His argument is as follows:

He dwells with no little amplification upon the 'introduction of the remarkable phrase,' 'ad disciplinam et regimen Ecclesiæ,' into the third chapter; that is, ' non solum in rebus quæ ad fidem et mores pertinent, sed etiam in iis quæ ad disciplinam et regimen Ecclesiæ per totum orbem diffusæ pertinent.' He says, 'Absolute obedience, it is boldly declared, is due to the Pope, at the peril of salvation, not only in faith and in morals, but in all things which concern the discipline and government of the Church' (p. 41). Submission in faith and morals is 'abject' enough, but 'in discipline and government' too is intolerable. 'Why did the astute contrivers of this tangled scheme, &c. . . . (p. 39). 'The work is now truly complete' (p. 40). This he calls 'the new version of the principles of the Papal Church.' When I read this, I asked, 'Is it possible that Mr. Gladstone should think this to be anything new? What does he conceive the Primacy of Rome to mean? With what eyes has he read history? Can he have read the tradition of the Catholic Church? As one of 'the astute contrivers,' I will answer that these words were introduced because the Pontiffs and Councils of the Church have always so used them. They may be 'remarkable' and 'new' to Mr. Gladstone, but they are old as the Catholic

Church. I give the first proofs which come to hand.

Nicholas I., in the year 863, in a Council at Rome, enacted: 'Si quis dogmata, mandata, interdicta, sanctiones vel decreta pro Catholica fide, pro ecclesiastica disciplina, pro correctione fidelium, pro emendatione sceleratorum, vel interdictione imminentium vel futurorum malorum, a Sedis Apostolicæ Præside salubriter promulgata contempserit: Anathema sit.'[1] This was an 'iron gripe' not less 'formidable' than the third chapter of the Vatican Constitution.

It may be said, perhaps, that this was only a Pontiff in his own cause; or only a Roman Council.

But this Canon was recognised in the Eighth General Council held at Constantinople in 869.[2]

Innocent III. may be no authority with Mr. Gladstone; but he says, what every Pontiff before him and after him has said, 'Nos qui sumus ad *regimen* Universalis Ecclesiæ, superna dispositione vocati.'[3]

Again, Sixtus IV., in 1471, writes: 'Ad Universalis Ecclesiæ *regimen* divina disponente clementia vocatis,'[4] &c.

If this be not enough, we have the Council of Florence, in 1442, defining of the Roman Pontiff that 'Ipsi in Beato Petro pascendi, *regendi* ac *gubernandi* Universalem Ecclesiam a Domino nostro Jesu Christo plenam potestam traditam esse.'[5]

---

[1] Labbe, *Concil.* tom. x. p. 238, ed. Ven. 1730.
[2] *Ibid.* tom. x. p. 633. See *Petri Privilegium*, 2nd part, p. 81.
[3] Corpus Juris Canon. *Decret. Greg.* lib. ii. cap. xiii. Novit.
[4] Corpus Juris Canon. *Extrav. Comm.* lib. i. tit. ix. cap. i.
[5] Labbe, *Concil.* tom. xviii. p. 527, ed. Ven. 1732.

Finally the Council of Trent says:—'Unde merito Pontifices Maximi pro Suprema potestate sibi in Ecclesia universa tradita,'[1] &c.

I refrain from quoting Canonists and Theologians who use this language as to regimen and discipline. It needed no astuteness to transcribe the well-known traditional language of the Catholic Church. It is as universal in our law books as the forms of the Courts at Westminster. The Vatican Council has left the authority of the Pontiff precisely where it found it. The whole, therefore, of Mr. Gladstone's argument falls with the misapprehension on which it was based.

What, then, is there new in the Vatican Council? What is to be thought of the rhetorical description of 'Merovingian monarchs and Carlovingian mayors,' but that the distinguished author is out of his depth? The Pope had at all times the power to rule the whole Church not only in faith and morals, but also in all things which pertain to discipline and government, and that whether infallibly or not.

Such is literally the only attempt made by Mr. Gladstone to justify his assertions. But what has this to do with Civil Allegiance? There is not a syllable on the subject, there is not a proposition which can be twisted or tortured into such a meaning. The government of the Church, as here spoken of, is purely and strictly the Spiritual government of souls, both pastors and people, as it was exercised in the first three hundred years before any Christian State existed.

But next, if the Vatican Council has not spoken of the Civil Powers, nevertheless it has defined that the

[1] Sess. xiv. cap. vii.

Pope, speaking *ex cathedra*, is infallible : this definition, by retrospective action, makes all Pontifical acts infallible, the Bull *Unam Sanctam* included; and, by prospective action, will make all similar acts in future binding upon the conscience.

Certainly this is true. But what is there new in this? The Vatican Council did not make the Pope infallible. Was he not infallible before the Council? He is, therefore, not more infallible after it than before. If a handful of writers, here and there, denied his infallibility, the whole Church affirmed it. Proof of this shall be given in its place. For the present, I affirm that all acts *ex cathedra*, such as the Bull *Unam Sanctam*, the Bull *Unigenitus*, the Bull *Auctorem Fidei*, and the like, were held to be infallible as fully before the Vatican Council as now.

To this it will be said, 'Be it so; but nobody was bound under Anathema to believe them.' I answer that it is not the Anathema that generates faith. The infallibility of the Head of the Church was a doctrine of Divine Faith before it was defined in 1870, and to deny it was held by grave authorities to be at least proximate to heresy, if not actually heretical.[1] The Vatican Council has put this beyond question; but it was never lawful to Catholics to deny the infallibility of a Pontifical act *ex cathedra*. It is from simple want of knowledge that men suppose every doctrine not defined to be an open question. The doctrine of the Infallibility of the Church has never been defined to this day. Will any man pretend that this is an open question among Catholics? The

[1] *Petri Privilegium*, part i. pp. 61-66, and notes.

infallibility of the Pope was likewise never defined, but it was never an open question. Even the Jansenists did not venture to deny it, and the evasion of some of them, who gave 'obsequious silence' instead of internal assent to Pontifical acts, was condemned by Clement XI. The definition of the Vatican Council has made no change whatsoever except in the case of those who denied or doubted of this doctrine. No difference, therefore, whatsoever has been made in the state of those who believed it. If the integrity of their civil allegiance was unimpeded before 1870, it is unimpeded now. But Mr. Gladstone admits that it was unimpeded before. His contention is that it is impeded now. But this is self-contradictory, for they believed the same doctrine of infallibility both then and now. If Mr. Gladstone means that the Vatican Council has made a difference for the few who denied the doctrine, and for the authors of *Janus* and *Quirinus*, and the professors of 'obsequious silence,' his contention is most true. But then he must change his whole position. The title of his pamphlet must be amended and stand, ' The Vatican Decrees in their Bearing on the Civil Allegiance of those who before 1870 denied the Infallibility of the Pope.' But this would ruin his case; for he would have admitted the loyalty of Catholics who always believed it before the definition was made.

We are next told that there are some twelve theories of what is an act *ex cathedra*. We have been also told that there are twenty. But how is it that Mr. Gladstone did not see that by this the whole force of his argument is shaken? If the definition has left it so uncertain what acts are, and what acts are not, *ex cathedra*, who shall hold himself bound to obedience? Are the eighty condemnations indicated in the Syllabus *ex cathedra*? By this showing it is 12 to 1 that they may not be. It is an axiom in morals '*Lex dubia non obligat*.' But if it be doubtful whether the Syllabus is *ex cathedra*, I am not bound to receive it with interior assent. Again, Mr. Gladstone thinks to aggravate the case by adding that the Pope is to be the ultimate judge of what acts are *ex cathedra*. And who else should be? *Ejus est interpretari cujus est condere* is a principle of all law. Mr. Gladstone has been acting upon it all his life. But, perhaps it may be said, why did not the Council put beyond doubt what acts are *ex cathedra*? Well, the Council has done so, as I hope to show; and has done it with as great precision as the subject matter will admit. It has given five tests, or conditions, by which an act *ex cathedra* may be distinguished.

But it may be said that doubts may still exist, and that doubts may still be raised as to this or that Pontifical act whether it be *ex cathedra* or not. Surely common sense would say, consult the authority which made the law; the legislator is always at hand, always ready to explain his own meaning, and to define the limits of his intention. If there be anything unreasonable in this, all jurisprudence, including the British Constitution, labours under the same uncertainty, or rather the same inevitable imperfection.

I am surprised that Mr. Gladstone should have quoted the second paragraph of the chapter in the Vatican Constitution; and that he should have passed over the fourth paragraph, in which there are indeed the words 'potestatis sæcularis placito.' This is the only recognition of secular powers in the whole Constitution. In that paragraph two things are affirmed: the one that the free exercise of the supreme Spiritual power of the Head of the Christian Church may neither be intercepted, nor hindered, nor excluded from any part of the Church by any human authority; and, secondly, that all such acts of his Spiritual power are valid and complete in themselves, and need, for that end, no confirmation or *placitum* of any other authority. This independence is claimed for Christianity by every one who believes in a revelation. Here is indeed a reference to Civil Powers; but, lest the Vatican Council should be held guilty of such innovations, I will add that such was the contention of St. Thomas of Canterbury against Henry II. in the case of the Constitutions of Clarendon, which were not 'cursed,' as Mr. Gladstone delicately expresses it, but condemned by Alexander III. in the year 1164. This, then, has not changed the Civil Allegiance of Catholics since 1870.

But I am not undertaking to prove a negative. I hope that I have shown that the evidence offered to prove that the Council has made the alleged change is *nil*. I affirm, then, once more that the Vatican Council has not touched the question of Civil Allegiance, that it has not by a jot or a tittle changed the relations in which the Church has ever stood to the Civil Powers; and that, therefore, the Civil Allegiance of Catholics is as full, perfect, and complete since the Council as it was before. These are affirmations capable of truth, and before I have done I hope to prove them. For the present it will be enough to give the reason why the Vatican Council did not touch the question of the relations of the Church to the Civil Powers. The reason is simple. *It intended not to touch them*, until it could treat them fully and as a whole. And it has carefully adhered to its intention. I will also give the reason why it has been so confidently asserted that the Council did touch the Civil Powers. It is because certain persons, a year before the Council met, resolved to say so. They wrote the book *Janus* to prove it; they published circulars and pamphlets before and during the Council to re-assert it. They first prophesied that the Council would interfere with the Civil Powers, and now they write scientific history to prove that it has done so. I am not writing at random; I carefully collected at the time their books, pamphlets, and articles. I read them punctually, and bound them up into volumes, which are now before me. Mr. Gladstone has reproduced their arguments. But for this systematic agitation before the Council, no one, I am convinced, would have found a shadow of cause for it in its Decrees. Now, that I may not seem to write this as prompted by the events of the present moment, I will repeat what I published in the year 1869, before the Council assembled, and in the year 1870, after the Council was suspended.

Before the Council met I published these words:[1]—

---

[1] 'The Œcumenical Council and the Infallibility of the Roman Pontiff,' *Petri Privilegium*, part ii. pp. 131–5. (Longmans, 1871.)

'Whilst I was writing these lines a document has appeared purporting to be the answers of the Theological Faculty of Munich to the questions of the Bavarian Government.

'The questions and the answers are so evidently concerted, if not written by the same hand, and the *animus* of the document so evidently hostile to the Holy See, and so visibly intended to create embarrassments for the supreme authority of the Church, both in respect to its past acts and also in respect to the future action of the Œcumenical Council, that I cannot pass it over. But, in speaking of it, I am compelled, for the first time, to break silence on a danger which has for some years been growing in its proportions, and, I fear I must add, in its attitude of menace. The answers of the University of Munich are visibly intended to excite fear and alarm in the Civil Powers of Europe, and thereby to obstruct the action of the Œcumenical Council if it should judge it to be opportune to define the Infallibility of the Pope. The answers are also intended to create an impression that the theological proofs of the doctrine are inadequate, and its definition beset with uncertainty and obscurity. In a word, the whole correspondence is a transparent effort to obstruct the freedom of the Œcumenical Council on the subject of the Infallibility of the Pontiff; or, if that doctrine be defined, to instigate the Civil Governments to assume a hostile attitude towards the Holy See. And this comes in the name of liberty, and from those who tell us that the Council will not be free.

'I shall take the liberty, without further words, of dismissing the Bavarian Government from our thoughts. But I must declare, with much regret, that this Munich document appears to me to be seditious.

'Facts like these give a certain warrant to the assertion and prophecies of politicians and Protestants. They prove that in the Catholic Church there is a school at variance with the doctrinal teaching of the Holy See in matters which are not of faith. But they do not reveal how small that school is. Its centre would seem to be at Munich. It has, both in France and England, a small number of adherents. They are active, they correspond, and for the most part write anonymously. It would be difficult to describe its tenets, for none of its followers seem to be agreed in all points. Some hold the Infalllibilty of the Pope, and some defend the Temporal Power. Nothing appears to be common to all, except an *animus* of opposition to the acts of the Holy See in matters outside the faith.

'In this country, about a year ago, an attempt was made to render impossible, as it was confidently but vainly thought, the definition of the Infallibility of the Pontiff by reviving the monotonous controversy about Pope Honorius. Later, we were told of I know not what combination of exalted personages in France for the same end. It is certain that these symptoms are not sporadic and disconnected, but in mutual understanding and with a common purpose. The anti-Catholic press has eagerly encouraged this school of thought. If a Catholic can be found out of tune with authority by half a note, he is at once extolled for unequalled learning and irrefragable logic. The anti-Catholic journals are at his service, and he vents his opposition to the common opinions of the Church by writing against them anonymously. Sad as this is, it is not formidable. It has effect almost alone upon those who are not Catholic. Upon Catholics its effect is hardly appreciable; on the Theological Schools of the Church it will have little influence; upon the Œcumenical Council it can have none.

'I can hardly persuade myself to believe that the University of Munich does not know that the relations between the Pope, even supposed to be infallible, and the Civil Powers have been long since precisely defined in the same acts which defined the relations between the Church, known to be infallible, and the Civil Authority. Twelve Synods or Councils, two of them Œcumenical, have long ago laid down these relations of the Spiritual and Civil Powers.[1] If the Pope were declared to be infallible to-morrow, it would in no way affect those relations.

'We may be sure . . . that this intellectual disaffection, of which, in these last days, we have had in France a new and mournful example, will have no influence upon either the Œcumenical Council or the policy of the Great Powers of Europe. They will not meddle with speculations of theological or historical critics. They know too well that they cannot do in the nineteenth century what was done in the sixteenth and the seventeenth.

'The attempt to put a pressure upon the General Council, if it have any effect upon those who are subject to certain governments, would have no effect but to rouse a just indignation in the Episcopate of the Church throughout the world. They hold their jurisdiction from a higher fountain, and they recognise no superior in their office of Judges of Doctrine, save only the Vicar of Jesus Christ. This preliminary meddling has already awakened a sense of profound responsibility and an inflexible resolution to allow no pressure or influence, or menace or intrigue, to cast so much as a shadow across their fidelity to the Divine Head of the Church and to His Vicar upon earth.

'Moreover, we live in days when the "Regium Placitum" and "Exequaturs" and "Arrêts" of Parliament in Spiritual things are simply dead. It may have been possible to hinder the promulgation of the Council of Trent; it is impossible to hinder the promulgation of the Council of the Vatican. The very liberty of which men are proud will publish it. Ten thousand presses in all lands will promulgate every act of the Church and of the Pontiff, in the face of all Civil Powers.

---

[1] Bellarm. *Opuscula adv. Barclaium*, p. 845, ed. Col. 1617.

Once published, these acts enter the domain of faith and conscience, and no human legislation, no civil authority, can efface them. The two hundred millions of Catholics will know the Decrees of the Vatican Council; and to know them is to obey. The Council will ask no civil enforcement, and it will need no civil aid. The Great Powers of Europe have long declared that the conscience of men is free from civil constraint. They will not stultify their own declarations by attempting to restrain the acts of the Vatican Council. The guardians and defenders of the principles of 1789 ought to rise as one man against all who should so violate the base of the political society in France. What attitude lesser Governments may take is of lesser moment.'

(2) I will now state positively what the Council has defined on the subject of the Roman Pontiff. The history then of the Definition of the Infallibility is as follows:—

1. Two *Schemata*, as they were called, or treatises, had been prepared: the one on the nature of the Church; the other on its relations to the Civil State.

The first alone came before the Council; the second has never yet been so much as discussed.

In the schema on the nature of the Church, its Infallibility was treated; but the Infallibility of its Head was not so much as mentioned. His Primacy and authority alone were treated. In the end, the chapter relating to the Primacy and authority was taken out, and subdivided into four. The subject of the Infallibility of the Roman Pontiff was then introduced.

The reasons for this change of order were given in 1870, as follows:—

In all theological treatises, excepting indeed one

or two of great authority, it had been usual to treat of the Body of the Church before treating of its Head. The reason of this would appear to be that in the exposition of doctrine the logical order was the more obvious; and to the faithful, in the first formation of the Church, the Body of the Church was known before its Head. We might have expected that the Council would have followed the same method. It is, therefore, all the more remarkable that the Council inverted that order, and defined the prerogative of the Head before it treated of the constitution and endowments of the Body. And this, which was brought about by the pressure of special events, is not without significance. The schools of the Church have followed the logical order; but the Church in Council, when for the first time it began to treat of its own constitution and authority, changed the method, and, like the Divine Architect of the Church, began in the historical order, with the foundation and Head of the Church. Our Divine Lord first chose Cephas, and invested him with the primacy over the Apostles. Upon this rock all were built, and from him the whole unity and authority of the Church took its rise. To Peter alone first was given the plenitude of jurisdiction and of infallible authority. Afterwards, the gift of the Holy Ghost was shared with him by all the Apostles. From him and through him therefore all began. For which cause a clear and precise conception of his Primacy and privilege is necessary to a clear and precise conception of the Church. Unless it be first distinctly apprehended, the doctrine of the Church will be always proportionately obscure. The doctrine of the Church does not determine the doctrine of the Primacy, but the doctrine of the Primacy does precisely determine the doctrine of the Church. In beginning, therefore, with the Head, the Council has followed our Lord's example, both in teaching and in fact; and in this will be found one of the causes of the singular and luminous precision with which the Council of the Vatican has, in one brief Constitution, excluded the well-known errors on the Primacy and Infallibility of the Roman Pontiff.

The reasons which prevailed to bring about this change of method were not only those which demonstrated generally the opportuneness of defining the doctrine, but those also which showed specially the necessity of bringing on the question while as yet the Council was in the fulness of its numbers. It was obvious that the length of time consumed in the discussion, reformation, and voting of the *Schemata* was such that, unless the Constitution *De Romano Pontifice* were brought on immediately after Easter, it could not be finished before the setting in of summer should compel the bishops to disperse. Once dispersed, it was obvious they could never again reassemble in so large a number. Many who with great earnestness desired to share the blessing and the grace of extinguishing the most dangerous error which for two centuries had disturbed and harassed the faithful, would have been compelled to go back to their distant sees and missions, never to return. It was obviously of the first moment that such a question should be discussed and decided, not, as we should have been told, in holes and corners, or by a handful of bishops, or by a faction, or by a clique, but by the largest possible assembly of the

Catholic Episcopate. All other questions, on which little divergence of opinion existed, might well be left to a smaller number of bishops; but a doctrine which for so long had vexed both pastors and people, the defining, not the truth, of which was contested by a numerous and organised opposition, needed to be treated and affirmed by the most extensive deliberation of the bishops of the Catholic Church. Add to this the many perils which hung over the continuance of the Council, of which I need but give one example. The outbreak of a war might have rendered the definition impossible. And in fact the Infallibility of the Roman Pontiff was defined on the eighteenth of July, and war was officially declared on the following day.

With these and many other contingencies fully before them, those who believed that the definition was, not only opportune, but necessary for the unity of the Church and of the Faith, urged its immediate discussion. Events justified their foresight. The debate was prolonged into the heats of July, when, by mutual consent, the opposing sides withdrew from a further prolonging of the contest, and closed the discussion. If it had not been already protracted beyond all limits of reasonable debate—for not less than a hundred fathers in the general and special discussions had spoken chiefly, if not alone, of Infallibility—it could not so have ended. Both sides were convinced that the matter was exhausted.[1]

2. In order to demonstrate, if possible, more abundantly that the Vatican Council has not so much as

---

[1] *Petri Privilegium*, part iii. pp. 51-54.

touched the relations of the Church to the Civil Power, I will give a brief analysis of its Definitions in what is called the First Dogmatic Constitution on the Church of Christ.

It is, as I have said, a portion of the Schema or treatise on the Church, taken out and enlarged into a Constitution by itself. There would have been only one Constitution treating of both the Body and the Head of the Church. Now there are two. The first, treating of the Head, has been completed; the second, treating of the Body, yet remains.

Now of the First Constitution there are four chapters.

The first treats of the Institution of the Apostolic Primacy in Saint Peter. The sum of it is that Our Lord appointed Peter to be Head of the whole Church, and gave him immediately a Primacy, not of honour only, but of jurisdiction. There is here not a word of anything but the Pastoral or Spiritual power.

The second declares the Primacy to be perpetual. It affirms two things: the one that Peter has a perpetual line of successors, and that the Roman Pontiff is the successor of Peter in that Primacy.

The third affirms the jurisdiction of the Roman Pontiff to be full and supreme in all things of faith and morals, and also in discipline and government of the Church; and that this jurisdiction is ordinary and immediate over all Churches and persons.

The fourth chapter treats of the Infallibility of the *Magisterium*, or the teaching authority of the Roman Pontiff. This chapter affirms that a Divine assistance was given to Peter, and in Peter to his successors for the discharge of their supreme office. It affirms also that this is a tradition received from the beginning of the Christian Faith. They, therefore, who tell us that the Vatican Council has brought in a new doctrine show that they do not know what the Vatican Council has said, and what it is that they must refute before their charge of innovation can be listened to.

Now it is to be observed:

1. That the Council declares that the Roman Pontiff, speaking *ex cathedra*, has a Divine assistance which preserves him from error.
2. That he speaks *ex cathedra* when he speaks under these five conditions: (1) as Supreme Teacher (2) to the whole Church. (3) Defining a doctrine (4) to be held by the whole Church (5) in faith and morals.

If disputants and controversialists had read and mastered these five conditions, we should have been spared much senseless clamour.

3. Lastly, it is to be observed that the Council has not defined the limit of the phrase 'faith and morals.' This well-known formula is plain and intelligible. The deposit committed to the Church is the Revelation of Divine Truth, and of the Divine Law. The Church is the guardian and witness, the interpreter and the expositor of the Truth and of the Law of God. Such is the meaning of 'faith and morals.' It is a formula well known, perfectly clear, sufficiently precise for our spiritual and moral life. If questions may be raised about the limits of faith and morals, it is because questions may be raised about anything; and questions will always be raised by those who love contention

against the Catholic Church more than they love either faith or morals. All argument against the Vatican Council as to the limits or extent of this formula is so much labour lost. It has not so much as touched the extent or the limits.

Such, then, is the whole of the first Constitution *De Ecclesia Christi*. It does not contain a syllable of the relation of this Primacy to the Civil or Political State, except to say that no human authority is needed for the validity of its acts, nor may any human power hinder their exercise. But these are truths as old as the day when St. Peter said before the council in Jerusalem, 'If it be just, in the sight of God, to hear you rather than God, judge ye.'[1] I hope, then, I have justified my assertion that the Vatican Council has not changed by a jot or a tittle the civil allegiance of Catholics. It is as free and perfect now as it was before.

As I have affirmed that the doctrine of the Infallibility of the Head of the Church was a doctrine of Divine Faith before the Council, and that the denial of it was confined to a small school of writers, I might be expected here to offer the historical proof of this assertion.

But I have already done so in the year 1869, before the Council assembled. I would therefore refer to the second part of 'Petri Privilegium'[2] for, as I believe, a sufficient proof. I will, however, in few words give the outline of what was then said.

It is acknowledged by the adversaries of the doctrine that from the Council of Constance in 1414 to

[1] Acts iv. 19.   [2] Part ii. pp. 63–107.

this day the doctrine has been the predominant belief of the Church. I gave evidence of its existence from the Council of Constance upwards to the Council of Chalcedon in 445.

Next I traced the history of the growth of the opinions adverse to the Infallibility of the Roman Pontiff from the Council of Constance to the year 1682, when it was, for the first time, reduced to formula by an assembly of French ecclesiastics under the influence of Louis XIV.

Lastly, I showed how this formula was no sooner published than it was condemned in every Catholic country by bishops and universities, and by the Holy See. The sum of the evidence for the first period was then given as follows:—

Gallicanism is no more than a transient and modern opinion, which arose in France, without warrant or antecedents in the ancient theological schools of the French Church; a royal theology, as suddenly developed and as parenthetical as the Thirty-nine Articles, affirmed only by a small number out of the numerous Episcopate of France, indignantly rejected by many of them; condemned in succession by three Pontiffs; declared by the Universities of Louvain and Douai to be erroneous; retracted by the bishops of France; condemned by Spain, Hungary, and other countries; and condemned over again in the Bull *Auctorem Fidei*.

From this evidence it is certain:—

    1. That Gallicanism has no warrant in the doctrinal practice or tradition of the Church, either in France or at large, in the thousand years preceding the Council of Constance.

2. That the first traces of Gallicanism are to be found about the time of that Council.
3. That after the Council of Constance they were rapidly and almost altogether effaced from the theology of the Church in France, until their revival in 1682.
4. That the Articles of 1682 were conceived by Jansenists, and carried through by political and oppressive means contrary to the sense of the Church in France.
5. That the theological faculties of the Sorbonne, and of France generally, nobly resisted and refused to teach them.[1]

But Gallicanism was the only formal interruption of the universal belief of the Church in the Infallibility of its Head. The Vatican Council extinguished this modern error.

II. Having thus far offered proof of the first proposition in my first letter, I will now go on to the second.

I there affirmed that the Civil Allegiance of Catholics is as undivided as that of all Christians, and of all men who recognise a divine or natural moral law.

Mr. Gladstone requires of us ' solid and undivided allegiance."[2]

I must confess to some surprise at this demand. The allegiance of every moral being is 'divided,' that is, twofold; not, indeed, in the same matter nor on the same plane, but in two spheres, and on a higher and a lower level, so that no collision is possible, except by

---

[1] *Petri Privilegium*, part ii. p. 56.   [2] P. 44.

some deviation or excess. Every moral being is under two authorities—human and divine. The child is under the authority of parents, and the authority of God; the subject is under the authority of the Civil State, and the Divine authority of natural or revealed religion. Unless we claim Infallibility for the State, its acts must be liable to revision, and to resistance by natural conscience. An unlimited obedience to parents or to States would generate a race of unlimited monsters. Surely these are truisms. Our Lord Himself taught this division when He said, ' Render therefore to Cæsar the things that are Cæsar's, and to God the things that are God's.' But this all men admit when they think. Unfortunately, when they attack the Catholic Church or the Vatican Council they seldom think much.

Put the objection in this form : ' We non-Catholics acknowledge two authorities as you Catholics do. Our allegiance to the civil law is revised and checked by our consciences, guided by the light of nature and by the light of revelation. We refuse to receive religious doctrine or discipline from the State. We allow the Society of Friends, for conscience sake, to refuse to take an oath of allegiance, and even to fight for their country, for conscience sake; and yet these two are among the natural duties of subjects which the civil authority may most justly both require and enforce. We therefore leave every man free to refuse obedience to civil laws if his conscience so demands of him. But you Catholics put your conscience into the hands of the Pope. You are bound to follow his interpretation of the civil law; and he tells you when your conscience ought to refuse obedience whether you see it or not; worse than this, the Pope may wrongly interpret our civil laws, or he may even so interpret them as to serve his own interests; and then your moral and mental freedom is at the mercy of another. You must choose between your religion and your country.' I think I have not understated the argument of our adversaries.

To this the answer is twofold. First, that the non-Catholic doctrine is more dangerous to the Civil State than the Catholic. If any individual conscience may dispense itself from civil obedience, then almost all men will obey only 'for wrath' and not for 'conscience sake.'[1] And such, in fact, is the condition of millions of men. I could wish that the mental state of the masses were better known. I wish it were possible to ascertain, by letting down a thermometer into the deep sea of our population, what notions remain of loyalty or allegiance. No doubt, in an insular population like ours, the traditional custom of inert conformity with law maintains a passive compliance which passes for Civil Allegiance. But take the population of countries where the so-called rights of the political conscience of individuals have had their legitimate development. A law is a law so far as it is accepted; a man is bound by the law so far as he had a hand in making it. If you once admit that the ultimate decision as to civil obedience is in the individual, each political conscience is a lawgiver and a law to itself. You cannot fly principles with a string as boys fly kites. Once enunciated

[1] Rom. xiii. 5.

they have nothing to control them. If every man has the ultimate right of refusing obedience to the law upon the dictates of his own conscience, then we are in a state of unlimited license, which is potentially a state of unlimited revolution. And such, in truth, since 1789 has been the state of the west of Europe. It is in a state of chronic instability and continuous change. More than forty revolutions have sprung from this essential lawlessness.

Secondly, according to the doctrine of the Catholic Church, the rights of individual conscience are secured not only against external coercion, but against its own aberrations. The obedience of Catholic subjects to their Civil Rulers is a positive precept of religion. The rising against legitimate authority is forbidden as the sin of rebellion. The Syllabus has condemned the propositions :—

> 'Authority is nothing else but the result of numerical superiority and material force.'— Prop. 60.
>
> 'It is allowable to refuse obedience to legitimate Princes, and also to rebel against them.'— Prop. 63.

The political conscience of Catholics is not left to the individual judgment alone. It is guided by the whole Christian morality, by the greatest system of ethical legislation the world has ever seen, the Canon Law and the Moral Theology of the Catholic Church. Not only all capricious and wilful resistances of the Civil Law, but all unreasonable and contentious disobedience is condemned by its authority. It is a doctrine of faith that legitimate sovereignty exists not only in the unity of the Church, but outside of the same; and not only among Christian nations, but also among the nations that are not Christian.[1] Moreover, that to all such legitimate sovereigns subjects are bound by the Divine Law[2] to render obedience in all lawful things. It is certain, threfore, that Catholics are bound to Civil Allegiance by every bond, natural and supernatural, as absolutely as their non-Catholic fellow-countrymen; and, I must add, more explicitly. And further, that they can hardly be reduced to the necessity of using their private judgment as to the lawfulness of obeying any law. In all matters of ordinary civil and political life, the duty of Catholics is already defined by a whole code which enforces obedience for conscience sake. In the rare case of doubt which may arise in times of religious persecution, political revolution, civil wars, or wars of succession, Catholic and non-Catholic subjects are alike in this,— they are both compelled to choose their side. But the non-Catholic subject has hardly law or judge to aid his conscience: the Catholic has both. He has the whole traditional moral law of Christendon, which has formed and perpetuated the civil and political order of the modern world, and he has a multitude of principles, maxims, and precedents on which to form his own judgment. Finally, if he be unable so to do, he can seek for guidance from an authority which the whole Christian world once believed to be the highest judicial tribunal and the source of its civil order and stability. And is this to place ' his mental and moral freedom at

---

[1] Rom. xiii. 1–4. [2] St. Peter ii. 13–15.

the mercy of another?' As much as and no more than we place ourselves 'at the mercy' of the Christian Church for our salvation. Let us take an example. It is certain, by the natural and Divine Law, that every man may defend himself, and that every people has the right of self-defence. On this all defensive wars are justifiable. But if the Sovereign levy war upon his people, have they the right of self-defence? Beyond all doubt. But at what point may they take up arms? and what amount of oppression justifies recourse to resistance? For the non-Catholics there can only be these answers. 'He must go by the light of his own conscience, or he must be guided by the judgment of the greater number, or by the wiser heads of his nation.' But the greater number may not be the wiser; and to judge who are the wiser throws the judgment once more upon himself. The Catholic subject would use his own judgment, and the judgment of his countrymen, but he would not hold himself at liberty to take up arms unless the Christian law confirmed the justice of his judgment. But from whom is this judgment to be sought? He would ask it of all those of whom he asks counsel in the salvation of his soul. If this is to be at the mercy of another, we are all at the mercy of those whom we believe to be wiser than ourselves.

Let us take an example. The Italian people have been for twenty years spectators of a revolution which has overthrown the Sovereigns of Naples and Tuscany. I will ask two questions. First, would any Italian place himself at the mercy of another, if he should ask of the head of his religion what course as a Christian he ought to pursue?

And, secondly, what has been the action of the Pope in respect to the Italian revolution? He has said that to co-operate in the Italian revolution is not lawful. Surely, if Italians are free to form their conscience on the doctrines of the revolution, they are equally free to form their conscience on the doctrines of their religion. To deny this is to have two weights and two measures. The non-Catholic theory tells us that the conscience of subjects is the ultimate test. Be it so; my conscience tells me that it is right to obey my religion rather than the revolution. If this be a divided allegiance, then it is Christianity which has introduced it, and not the Church. It was our Lord Himself who, by instituting His Church, separated for ever the two powers, Civil and Spiritual, thereby redeeming the conscience and the religion of men from the dominion of princes, and conferring upon the Civil Power the consecration by which it is confirmed, and the higher law by which its sphere is defined. It is all this, and not[1] 'our old friend the deposing power alone,' which I have described as teaching obedience to subjects and moderation to princes.[2] In all conflicts between the Civil and Spiritual, the consciences of Christians will be decided by the Christian law.

I conclude, therefore, this part of the subject by reasserting:—

1. That the relations of the Church to the State

---

[1] *Expostulation*, p. 52.
[2] *Temporal Power of the Pope*, pp. 44–46, second ed. 1862.

were never so much as proposed for discussion in the Vatican Council.

2. That in its Constitutions or Definitions it has in no way touched the subject.

3. That the Definitions of the Council are 'declaratory' of doctrine already of Divine Faith, and that no new 'enactment' whatsoever was made.

4. That the relations of the Church to the Civil Power were left by the Vatican Council as they were known and declared by the Council of Trent and all previous Councils.

I will therefore answer Mr. Gladstone's questions in page 44 of his 'Expostulation.' He tells us that 'what is not wanted is vague and general assertion of whatever kind, and howsoever sincere. What is wanted, and that in the most specific form and in the clearest terms, I take to be one of two things, that is to say, either—

'1. A demonstration that neither in the name of faith, nor in the name of morals, nor in the name of the government or discipline of the Church, is the Pope of Rome able, by virtue of the powers asserted for him by the Vatican decree, to make any claim upon those who adhere to his communion of such a nature as can impair the integrity of their Civil allegiance; or else,

'2. That if, and when such claim is made, it will even, although resting on the definitions of the Vatican, be repelled and rejected.'[1]

I have shown that the Pope is not able, by the Vatican Council, to make any claim in the name of

---

[1] *The Vatican Decrees*, p. 44.

faith, nor in the name of morals, nor in the name of the government or discipline of the Church, which he was not able to make before the Vatican Council existed.

To Mr. Gladstone's first question, therefore, I answer, that neither in virtue of the Vatican Decrees, nor of any other decrees, nor of his supreme authority as Head of the Christian Church, can the Pope make any claim upon those who adhere to his communion of such a nature as can impair the integrity of their Civil Allegiance.

To his second question, therefore, the answer is already given. I have no need to declare myself ready to repel and reject that which the Pope cannot do. He cannot do an act contrary to the Divine Law; but to impair my Civil Allegiance would be contrary to the Law of God.

It is strange to me that so acute a reasoner should have begged the question, which is this: By whom are the limits of Civil Allegiance to be determined? If Mr. Gladstone should say by the State, I would ask —Does he mean that the State is infallible in morals? or that subjects have no conscience, or that the State may coerce their conscience, or that the State can create a morality which all consciences must obey? Some of these postulates are inevitably assumed in his question, if it has any meaning.

My reasons for saying this will be seen in the following chapter.

CHAPTER II.

THE RELATIONS OF THE SPIRITUAL AND CIVIL POWERS.

WE will now go on to my second proposition, that the relations of the Catholic Church to the Civil Powers have been fixed immutably from the beginning, because they arise out of the Divine constitution of the Church and out of the Civil Society of the natural order.

I. Inasmuch as the natural and civil society existed before the foundation of the Christian Church, we will begin with it; and here my concessions, or rather my assertions, will, I hope, satisfy all but Cæsarists.

1. The civil society of men has God for its Founder. It was created potentially in the creation of man; and from him has been unfolded into actual existence. The human family contains the first principles and laws of authority, obedience, and order. These three conditions of society are of Divine origin; and they are the constructive laws of all civil or political society.

2. To the Civil Society of mankind supreme authority is given *immediately* by God; for a society does not signify mere number, but number organised by the laws and principles which its Divine Founder implanted in the human family. Sovereignty, therefore, is given by God immediately to human society; and *mediately*, or *mediante societate*, to the person or persons to

whom society may commit its custody and its exercise.
When once the supreme power or sovereignty has been
committed by any society to a king, or to consuls, or
to a council, as the case may be—for God has given no
special form of Civil Government—though it be not
held by those who receive it by any Divine right, as
against the society which gave it, nevertheless it has
both a Divine sanction and a Divine authority. For
instance, it has the power of life and death. God
alone could give to man this power over man. God
gave it to man for self-defence. It passes to society at
large, which likewise has the right of self-defence. It
is committed by society to its chief executive. But,
inasmuch as the supreme power is still given by God
to the Civil Ruler, even though it be *mediately*, it has
a Divine sanction; and so long as the Civil Ruler does
not deviate from the end of his existence, the society
has no power to revoke its act. For example: the
Civil Ruler is for the defence of the people; but if he
should make war upon the people, the right of self-defence would justify resistance. I am not now engaged
in saying when or how; but the right is undeniable.
Manslaughter is not murder, if it be in self-defence;
wars of defence are lawful; and just resistance to an
unjust prince is not rebellion. All this is founded
upon the Divine sanctions of the civil and political
society of man, even in the order of nature. It has,
then, God for its Founder, for its Legislator, and by
His divine Providence for its supreme Ruler.

3. The laws of such society are the laws of nature. It
is bound by the natural morality written on the conscience and on the heart. The ethics which govern

men become politics in the government of states. Politics are but the collective morals of society. The Civil Ruler or Sovereign is bound by the laws: the subject within the sphere of these laws owes to him a civil allegiance. The Civil Ruler may bind all subjects by an oath of allegiance. He may call on all to bear arms for the safety of the State.

4. The State has for its end, not only the safety of person and property, but, in its fullest sense, the temporal happiness of man. Within the sphere of natural morality, and in order to its end, the State is supreme: and its power is from God. This is the meaning of St. Paul's words:—

'Let every soul be subject to higher powers: for there is no power but from God; and those that are, are ordained of God. Therefore he that resisteth the power, resisteth the ordinance of God; and they that resist, purchase to themselves damnation. . . . For he is God's minister to thee for good. But if thou do that which is evil, fear, for he beareth not the sword in vain: for he is God's minister, an avenger to execute wrath upon him that doeth evil. Wherefore be subject of necessity, not only for wrath but also for conscience sake.'[1]

The State, then, is a perfect society, supreme within its own sphere, and in order to its own end: but as that end is not the highest end of man, so the State is not the highest society among men; nor is it, beyond its own sphere and end, supreme. I have drawn this out in greater fulness to show that the Church is in the highest degree conservative of all the natural authority of rulers, and of the natural allegiance of

[1] Romans xiii. 1–5.

subjects. It is mere shallowness to say that between the Civil authority, as Divinely founded in nature, and the spiritual authority of the Church there can be opposition.

Now, as to the Divine institution of the Civil Society of the world and of its independence in all things of the natural order, what I have already said is enough. The laws of the order of nature are from God. So long as a father exercises his domestic authority according to the law of God, no other authority can intervene to control or to hinder his government. So likewise of the Prince or Sovereign power, be it lodged in one or in many. There is no authority upon earth which can depose a just sovereign or release such subjects from their obedience.[1]

II. There is, however, another society, the end of which is the eternal happiness of mankind. This also has God for its Founder, and that immediately; and it has received from God its form and constitution, and its rulers receive their authority immediately,[2] with a special Divine sanction and authority, from God.

Two things follow at once from this:—

1. That the society which has for its end the eternal happiness of man is of an order higher than the society which aims only at the natural happiness of man.
2. That as the temporal and the eternal happiness of man are both ordered by Divine laws, these two societies are, of necessity, in essen-

---

[1] 'Etiam nocentium potestas non est nisi a Deo.'—St. Augustine, *De Natura Boni contra Manich.* cap. xxxii.

[2] Suarez, *Defensio Fidei*, lib. iii. cap. ii. sect. 5, 15, 16.

tial conformity and harmony with each other. Collision between them can only be if either deviates from its respective laws.

The natural society of man aims *directly* at the temporal happiness of its subjects, but *indirectly* it aims also at their eternal happiness: the supernatural society aims *directly* at their eternal happiness, and *indirectly* at their temporal happiness, but always in so far only as their temporal happiness is conducive to their eternal end.

From this again two other corollaries follow:—

1. That the higher or supernatural society is supreme because it has no other society, above it or beyond it, with an end higher than its own.
2. That the office of the supernatural society is to aid, direct, and perfect the natural society; that its action upon it is always *in ædificationem non in destructionem*, inasmuch as it is governed by the same Divine Lawgiver, and it is directed to an end which includes and ensures the end of the natural society also.

To put this briefly. The State has for its end the temporal happiness of its subjects; the Church has for its end their eternal happiness. In aiming directly at temporal happiness, the State aims also indirectly at the eternal; for these things are promoted by the same laws. In aiming at eternal happiness, the Church also indirectly aims at the temporal happiness of men.

III. The Divine Founder of the Christian Church said: 'To thee I will give the keys of the kingdom of heaven. And whatsoever thou shalt bind on earth shall be bound also in heaven, and whatsoever thou shalt loose on earth shall be loosed also in heaven.'[1] And again: 'All power is given to me in heaven and in earth. Going therefore, teach all nations,' ... 'teaching them to observe all things whatsoever I have commanded you.'[2]

If these two commissions do not confer upon the Christian Church a supreme doctrinal authority, and a supreme judicial office, in respect to the moral law, over all nations, and over all persons, both governors and governed, I know not what words could suffice to do so.

That authority and that office are directive and preceptive, so long as Princes and their laws are in conformity with the Christian law; and judicial, *ratione peccati*, by reason of sin, whensoever they deviate from it.

If any man deny this, he would thereby affirm that Princes have no superior upon earth: which is the doctrine of the heathen Cæsarism.

But no man will say that Princes have no superior. It is unmeaning to say that they have no superior but the law of God: for that is to play with words. A law is no superior without an authority to judge and to apply it.

To say that God is the sole Lawgiver of Princes is a doctrine unknown, not only to the Catholic Church, but to the Constitution of England. When we say, as our old Jurists do, *Non Rex facit legem*, but *Lex facit Regem*, we mean that there is a will above the King; an that will

---

[1] St. Matthew xvi. 19.   [2] Ibid. xxviii. 18, 19.

is the Civil Society, who judges if and when the King deviates from the law. But this doctrine, unless it be tempered by vigorous restraint, is chronic revolution. What adequate restraint is there but in a Divine authority higher than the natural society of man?

The Supreme Judicial Power of the Church has no jurisdiction over those that are not Christian; and the entire weight of its authority, if it were applied at all to such a state, would be applied to confirm the natural rights of sovereignty and to enforce the natural duty of allegiance: and that, upon the principle that the supernatural power of the Church is for edification, not for destruction; that is, to build up and to perfect the order of nature, not to pull down a stone in the symmetry of the natural society of man. St. Thomas says:

'Power and authority are established by human right; the distinction between the faithful and those who do not believe is established by Divine right. But the Divine right, which comes by grace, does not destroy the human right, which is in the order of nature.'[1]

Let us suppose that the Sovereign Power of a heathen people were to make laws contrary to the law of God, would the Church intervene to depose such a sovereign? Certainly not, on the principle laid down by the Apostle, 'What have I to do to judge those that are without?'[2]

Such a people is both individually and socially outside the Divine jurisdiction of the Church. The Church

---

[1] St. Thomas, 2da 2dæ, quæst. x. art. 10.
[2] 1 Cor. v. 12.

has, therefore, in this respect, no commission to discharge towards it except to convert it to Christianity.

But if it be the office of the Church to teach subjects to obey even Heathen Rulers, as the Apostle did, how much more, in the case of Christian Princes and their laws, is it the office of the Church to confirm, consecrate, and enforce the sanctions of religion and of conscience, of doctrine and of discipline, the whole code of natural and political morality, and all laws that are made in conformity with the same.

If Christian Princes and their laws deviate from the law of God, the Church has authority from God to judge of that deviation, and by all its powers to enforce the correction of that departure from justice. I do not see how any man who believes in the Revelation of Christianity can dispute this assertion: and to such alone I am at present speaking.

Mr. Gladstone has quoted a passage from an 'Essay on Cæsarism and Ultramontanism,' in which I have claimed for the Church a supremacy in spiritual things over the State, and have made this statement:

'Any power which is independent and can alone fix the limits of its own jurisdiction, and can thereby fix the limits of all other jurisdictions, is, *ipso facto*, supreme. But the Church of Jesus Christ, within the sphere of revelation—of faith and morals—is all this, or is nothing or worse than nothing, an imposture and an usurpation; that is, it is Christ or Antichrist.'[1]

It is hardly loyal to take the conclusion of a syllogism without the premises. In the very page before this quotation I had said:

[1] *Cæsarism and Ultramontanism*, p. 36.

'In any question as to the competence of the two powers, either there must be some judge to decide what does and what does not fall within their respective spheres, or they are delivered over to perpetual doubt and to perpetual conflict. But who can define what is or is not within the jurisdiction of the Church in faith and morals, except a judge who knows what the sphere of faith and morals contains, and how far it extends? And surely it is not enough that such a judge should guess or opine, or pronounce upon doubtful evidence, or with an uncertain knowledge. Such a sentence would be, not an end of contention, but a beginning and a renewal of strife.

'It is clear that the Civil Power cannot define how far the circumference of faith and morals extends. If it could, it would be invested with one of the supernatural endowments of the Church. To do this it must know the whole deposit of explicit and implicit faith; or, in other words, it must be the guardian of the Christian revelation. Now, no Christian, nor any man of sound mind, claims this for the Civil Power. .... If, then, the Civil Power be not competent to decide the limits of the Spiritual Power, and if the Spiritual Power can define with a Divine certainty its own limits, it is evidently supreme. Or, in other words, the Spiritual Power knows with Divine certainty the limits of its own jurisdiction; and it knows therefore the limits and the competence of the Civil Power. It is thereby in matters of religion and conscience supreme.'[1]

If the Church cannot fix the limits of its jurisdiction, then either nobody can or the State must. But the State cannot unless it claim to be the depository and expositor of the Christian Revelation. Therefore it is the Church or nobody. This last supposition leads to chaos. Now if this be rejected, the

[1] *Cæsarism and Ultramontanism*, pp. 24, 35.

Church alone can: and if the Church can fix the limits of its own jurisdiction, it can fix the limits of all other jurisdiction; at least, so far as to warn it off its own domain. But this was my conclusion; and though I have seen it held up to odium, I have not yet seen it answered.

But the Church being the highest society, and independent of all others, is supreme over them, in so far as the eternal happiness of man is involved.

From this, again, two consequences follow:—

1. First, that in all things which are purely temporal, and lie *extra finem Ecclesiæ*, outside of the end of the Church, it neither claims nor has jurisdiction.
2. Secondly, that in all things which promote, or hinder, the eternal happiness of men, the Church has a power to judge and to enforce.

IV. Such propositions are no sooner enunciated than we are met by a tumult of voices, such as those of *Janus*, *Quirinus*—and I lament to detect the tones of a voice, hitherto heard in behalf of the authority of Christianity and of the Christian Church,—affirming that the Church of Rome and its Pontiffs claim supreme temporal[1] power, and that direct, over all Temporal Princes and things; to be used at their discretion even to the deposing of Kings, to the absolution of subjects from allegiance, to the employment of force, imprisonment, torture, and death.

If such be the state of our highest minds, we cannot regret that this discussion has been forced upon us.

[1] *Expostulation*, p. 27.

It has come not by our act. It has arisen in its time appointed. It will for awhile raise alarm and suspicion; it will kindle animosity and encourage bigotry: but it will manifest the truth with a wider light than England has seen for three hundred years. I will therefore freely and frankly enter upon this debate, and, in order to be clear, I will treat the subject under the following propositions :—

1. The authority of Princes and the allegiance of subjects in the Civil State of nature is of Divine ordinance; and, therefore, so long as Princes and their laws are in conformity to the law of God, the Church has no power or jurisdiction against them, nor over them.

2. If Princes and their laws deviate from the law of God, the Church has authority from God to judge of that deviation, and to oblige to its correction.

3. The authority which the Church has from God for this end is not *temporal*, but *spiritual*.

4. This spiritual authority is not direct in its incidence on temporal things, but only indirect: that is to say, it *directly* promotes its own *spiritual* end; it *indirectly* condemns and declares not binding on the conscience such *temporal* laws as deviate from the law of God, and therefore impede or render impossible the attainment of the eternal happiness of man.

5. This spiritual authority is inherent in the Divine constitution and commission of the Church; but its exercise in the world depends on certain moral and material conditions, by which

alone its exercise is rendered either possible or just.

I have affirmed that the relations of the Catholic Church to the Civil Powers are fixed primarily by the Divine constitution of the Church and of the Civil Society of men. But it is also true that these relations have been declared by the Church in acts and decrees which are of infallible authority. Such, for instance, is the Bull of Boniface VIII., *Unam Sanctam.* As this has become the text and centre of the whole controversy at this moment, we will fully treat of it. This Bull, then, was beyond all doubt an act *ex cathedra.* It was also confirmed by Leo X. in the Fifth Lateran Œcumenical Council. Whatever definition, therefore, is to be found in this Bull is to be received as of faith. Let it be noted that the *Unam Sanctam* does not depend upon the Vatican Council for its infallible authority. It was from the date of its publication an infallible act, obliging all Catholics to receive it with interior assent. Doctrines identical with those of the *Unam Sanctam* had been declared in two Œcumenical Councils—namely, in the Fourth Lateran in 1215, and the First of Lyons in 1245.[1] On this ground, therefore, I have affirmed that the relations of the Spiritual and Civil Powers were immutably fixed before the Vatican Council met, and that they have been in no way changed by it.

V. We will now examine, (1) the complete text of the *Unam Sanctam ;* (2) the interpretations of its assail-

---

[1] Bellarmin. *De Potest. Papa.* in præf, p. 844, Cologne, 1617.

ants and its defenders; (3) the interpretation which is of obligation on all Catholics.

1. The Bull was published by Boniface VIII., in 1302, during the contest with Philip le Bel of France. Before the Bull was published, the Regalists or partisans of the King declared that the Pope had claimed, as Mr. Gladstone also supposes, to be supreme over the King, both in spiritual and in temporal things. The Chancellor Flotte made this assertion in the year 1301, at Paris, in the Church of Notre Dame. The cardinals sent by Boniface declared that the Pope made no such claim; that he claimed no temporal, but only a spiritual power.[1] Nevertheless, this prejudice, once created, before the publication of the *Unam Sanctam*, ensured its being misinterpreted when it was issued. Boniface, by the Bull *Ausculta Fili*, had promptly exposed this misinterpretation. But the prejudice was already established.[2]

I will now give the whole text of the Bull, before commenting upon it. It runs as follows :—

'We are bound to believe and to hold, by the obligation of faith, one Holy Church, Catholic and also Apostolic; and this (Church) we firmly believe and in simplicity confess: out of which there is neither salvation nor remission of sins. As the Bridegroom declares in the Canticles, "One is my dove, my perfect one, she is the only one of her mother, the chosen of her that bore her;"[3] who represents the one mystical Body, the Head of which is Christ; and the Head of Christ is God.

---

[1] Döllinger's *Church History*, vol. iv. p. 90.
[2] *Ibid.* p. 91.   [3] Cant. vi. 8.

In which (the one Church) there is one Lord, one Faith, one Baptism.[1] For in the time of the Flood the ark of Noe was one, prefiguring the one Church, which was finished in one cubit,[2] and had one governor and ruler, that is Noe; outside of which we read that all things subsisting upon earth were destroyed. This also we venerate as one, as the Lord says in the Prophet, " Deliver, O God, my soul from the sword: my only one from the hand of the dog."[3]

'For He prayed for the soul, that is, for Himself; for the Head together with the Body: by which Body he designated the one only Church, because of the unity of the Bridegroom, of the Faith, of the Sacraments, and of the charity of the Church. This is that coat of the Lord without seam,[4] which was not rent, but went by lots. Therefore of that one and only Church there is one body and one Head, not two heads as of a monster : namely, Christ and Christ's Vicar, Peter and Peter's successor; for the Lord Himself said to Peter, " Feed my sheep."[5] Mine, he says generally; and not, in particular, these or those : by which He is known to have committed all to him. If, therefore, Greeks or others say that they were not committed to Peter and his successors, they must necessarily confess that they are not of the sheep of Christ, for the Lord said (in the Gospel) by John, that there is " One fold, and one only shepherd."[6] By the words of the Gospel we are instructed that in this his (that is Peter's) power there are two swords, the spiritual and the temporal. For when the Apostles say, " Behold, here are two swords," that is,[7] in the Church, the Lord did not say, " It is too much," but " it is enough." Assuredly, he who denies that the temporal sword is in the power of Peter, gives ill heed to the word of the Lord, saying,

---

[1] Ephesians iv. 5. [2] Genesis vi. 16. [3] Psalm xxi. 21.
[4] St. John xix. 23, 24. [5] St. John xxi. 17. [6] St. John x. 16.
[7] St. Luke xxii. 38.

"Put up again thy sword into its place."[1] Both, therefore, the spiritual sword and the material sword are in the power of the Church. But the latter (the material sword) is to be wielded ON BEHALF OF the Church; the former (the spiritual) is to be wielded BY the Church: the one by the hand of the priest; the other by the hand of kings and soldiers, but at the suggestion and sufferance of the priest. The one sword ought to be subject to the other, and the temporal authority ought to be subject to the spiritual power. For whereas the Apostle says, "There is no power but from God; and those that are, are ordained of God;"[2] they would not be ordained (or ordered) if one sword were not subject to the other, and as the inferior directed by the other to the highest end. For, according to the blessed Dionysius, it is the law of the Divine order that the lowest should be guided to the highest by those that are intermediate. Therefore, according to the order of the universe, all things are not in equal and immediate subordination; but the lowest things are set in order by things intermediate, and things inferior by things superior. We ought, therefore, as clearly to confess that the spiritual power, both in dignity and excellence, exceeds any earthly power, in proportion as spiritual things are better than things temporal. This we see clearly from the giving, and blessing, and sanctifying of tithes, from the reception of the power itself, and from the government of the same things. For, as the truth bears witness, the spiritual power has to instruct, and judge the earthly power, if it be not good; and thus the prophecy of Jeremias is verified of the Church and the ecclesiastical power: "Lo, I have set thee this day over the nations and over kingdoms," etc.[3] If, therefore, the earthly power deviates (from its end), it will be judged by the spiritual; but if a lesser spiritual power transgresses, it will be judged by its superior;

[1] St. Matthew xxvi. 52.   [2] Romans xiii. 1.   [3] Jeremiah i. 10.

but if the supreme (deviates), it can be judged, not by man, but by God alone, according to the words of the Apostle: "The spiritual man judges all things; he himself is judged by no one." [1] This authority, though given to man and exercised through man, is not human, but rather Divine—given by the Divine voice to Peter, and confirmed to him and his successors in Him whom Peter confessed, the Rock, for the Lord said to Peter: "Whatsoever thou shalt bind upon earth, it shall be bound also in heaven: and whatsoever thou shalt loose on earth, it shall be loosed also in heaven." [2]

'Whosoever therefore resists this power that is so ordered by God, resists the ordinance of God,[3] unless, as Manichæus did, he feign to himself two principles, which we condemn as false and heretical; for, as Moses witnesses, "God created heaven and earth not in the beginnings, but in the beginning." [4] Moreover, we declare, affirm, define, and pronounce it to be necessary to salvation for every human creature to be subject to the Roman Pontiff.'

2. We will next take the interpretations. They may be put into three classes:—

(1) First, of those who assailed it at the time.

The theologians and doctors of the school at Paris had always taught by a constant tradition that the Popes possessed a spiritual and indirect power over temporal things. John Gerson may be taken as the representative of them all. He says the ecclesiastical power does not possess the dominion and the rights of earthly and of heavenly empire, so that it may dispose at will of the goods of the clergy, and much less of the laity; though it must be conceded that it has

---

[1] 1 Corinthians ii. 15.   [2] St. Matthew xvi. 19.
[3] Romans xiii. 2.   [4] Genesis i. 1.

in these thing an authority (*dominium*) to rule, to direct, to regulate, and to ordain.¹ Such was the doctrine of Almain, Alliacus, John of Paris, and of the old Sorbonne. It was also the doctrine of the theologians of the Council of Constance; who are always quoted as opponents of the Infallibility of the Pope, because they held that, though the See of Rome could not err, he that sat in it might err. They likewise held the deposing power, which alone is enough to show how little the definition of the Infallibility has to do with the deposition of Kings.

When the *Unam Sanctam* was published, Egidius Romanus, the Archbishop of Bourges, wrote against it, being deceived into a belief that Boniface claimed a direct temporal power over the King of France, over and above that power which had always been admitted in France according to the Bull *Novit* of Innocent III.— viz. an indirect spiritual power in temporal matters when involving sin.² The same course was taken by other French writers.

Boniface had already declared in a Consistory in 1302 that he had never assumed any jurisdiction which belonged to the King; but that he had declared the King to be, like any other Christian, subject to him only in regard to sin.

(2) Secondly, the Regalists once more assailed the *Unam Sanctam* in the reign of Louis XIV.

Bianchi says that there is not to be found a writer in

---

[1] Joann. Gerson, *De Potest. Eccles.* Consid. xii. Bianchi *Della Potestà et della Politia della Chiesa*, tom. i. lib. i. cap. xi.

[2] Bianchi, lib. i. cap. x.

[3] Döllinger's *History of the Church*, vol. iv. p. 91.

France, before Calvin, who denied this indirect spiritual power; that the denial was introduced by the Huguenots about the year 1626; that the Sorbonne began to adhere to it, and reduced it to a formula in 1662. Bossuet endeavours to fasten on the *Unam Sanctam* the old Regalist interpretation, and affirms that it was withdrawn by Clement V.: which statement is contrary to the fact. Clement V., on the contrary, interprets the Bull in the true sense, as Boniface had done, declaring that Boniface did not thereby subject the King, or the Kingdom of France, in any greater degree to the authority of the Pontiff than they had been before, that is, according to the Bull of Innocent III. *Novit*, and the doctrines of the old Sorbonne.[2]

The history of the Four Gallican Articles, and of the writers who defended them, is too well known to need repetition.

(3) We come, lastly, to those who have assailed it at this time.

It is not a little wearisome to read the same old stories over again; and to be told as 'scientific history' that Boniface VIII. claimed to have received both swords as his own, to be held in his own hand, and wielded by him in direct temporal jurisdiction over temporal princes. We have all this raked up again in *Janus*. From *Janus* it goes to newspapers, magazines, and pamphlets. Anybody can interpret a Pope's Bull. There is no need of a knowledge of contemporary facts, or of the terminology of the Civil or Canon

---

[1] Lib. i. cap. xiii.
[2] In the Appendix A will be found in full the Text of the three Pontifical Acts, *Novit, Unam Sanctam, Meruit*.

Law, or of Pontifical Acts, or of the technical meaning of words. A dictionary, and a stout heart to attack the Popes, is enough. Such men would have us believe, against all the Popes, that they have claimed temporal power, properly so called, over temporal Princes.

VI. I will, therefore, now give what may be affirmed to be the true and legitimate interpretation of the *Unam Sanctam*.

It cannot be better stated than in the words of Dr. Döllinger.[1] He writes thus:—

'Boniface opened the council, at which there were present from France four archbishops, thirty-five bishops, and six abbots, in November 1302. One consequence of this council appears to have been the celebrated decretal *Unam Sanctam*, which was made public on the 18th of November, and which contains an exposition of the relations between the spiritual and temporal powers. In the Church, it says, there are two powers, a temporal and spiritual, and as far as they are both in the Church, they have both the same end: the temporal power, the inferior, is subject to the spiritual, the higher and more noble; the former must be guided and directed by the latter, as the body is by the soul; it receives from the spiritual its consecration and its direction to its highest object, and must therefore, should it ever depart from its destined path, be corrected by the spiritual power. It is a truth of faith that all men, even kings, are subject to the Pope; if, therefore, they should be guilty of grievous sins, in peace or in war, or in the government of their kingdoms, and the treatment of their subjects, and should thus lose sight of the object to which the power of a Christian Prince should be directed, and should give public scandal to the people, the Pope can admonish them,

[1] *Hist.* iv. p. 91.

since in regard to sin they are subject to the spiritual power; he can correct them; and, if necessity should require it, compel them by censures to remove such scandals. For if they were not subject to the censures of the Church, whenever they might sin in the exercise of the power entrusted to them, it would follow that as kings they were out of the Church; that the two powers would be totally distinct from each other; and that they were descended from distinct and even opposed principles, which would be an error approaching to the heresy of the Manichees. It was therefore the indirect power of the Church over the temporal power of kings which the Pope defended in these Bulls; and he had designedly extracted the strongest passages of them from the writings of two French theologians, St. Bernard and Hugo of St. Victor.'

The interpretation given here by Dr. Döllinger is undoubtedly correct. All Catholics are bound to assent to the doctrines here declared; for though they are not here defined, yet they are certainly true. The only definition, properly so called, in the Bull is contained in the last sentence.

Now, upon the doctrines declared by the Bull it is to be observed :—

1. That it does not say that the two swords were *given* by our Lord to the Church; but that the two swords are *in potestate Ecclesiæ*, 'in the power of the Church.'
2. That it at once goes on to distinguish, ' Both (swords) are *in the power* of the Church, the spiritual, that is, and the material. But this (the material) is to be used *for* the Church; that (the spiritual) is to be used *by* the Church. This, indeed (by the hand) of the

Priest; that, by the hand of kings and soldiers, but at the bidding and sufferance of the Priest.'

3. That though both swords are *in* the Church, they are held in different hands, and to be used by the subordination of the one to the other. *Oportet autem gladium esse sub gladio:* the one sword must be subordinate to the other, the lower to the higher.

4. That Boniface VIII., in this very Bull *Unam Sanctam*, expressly declares that the power given to Peter was the '*Suprema Spiritualis potestas*,' not the Temporal, or a mixed power, but purely Spiritual, which may judge all Powers, but itself is judged of God alone.

Now, on the principles already laid down, there ought to be no difficulty in rightly and clearly understanding this doctrine.

1. For first the Material Sword is as old as human society. It was not given by grace, nor held by grace, which is a heresy condemned in Wiclif by the Council of Constance; but it belongs to the Civil Ruler in the order of nature, as St. Paul, speaking of the heathen empire, says: ' He beareth not the sword in vain; for he is the minister of God to execute wrath.'

Nothing but want of care or thought could have led men to forget this, which is a truth and fact of the natural order.

When any prince by baptism became Christian, he became subject to the law of God and to the

Church as its expositor. He became subject, not only as a man, but as a prince; not only in the duties of his private life, but in the duties of his public life also. But this did not deprive him of the civil sword, nor of any of the rights of the natural order.' *Oportet autem gladium esse sub gladio.* The Bull declares that the Material Sword which he brought with him when he was baptized ought to be subject to the Spiritual Sword. But it nowhere says that the Material Sword was given to the Church, or that the Church gave it to the Imperial Ruler. It is *in* the Church, because he that bears it is in the Church. It is the office of the Church to consecrate it, and (*instituere*) to *instruct* it. But it belongs essentially to the natural order, though it is to be exercised according to the supernatural order of faith.

 2. When it is said that both Swords are 'in *the power of the Church,*' it means that the Church in a Christian world includes the natural order in its unity. The conception of the Church included the whole complex Christian Society, made up of both powers, united in a complete visible unity.

Mr. Bryce, in his excellent work on the Holy Roman Empire, says:—

'Thus the Holy Roman Church and the Holy Roman Empire are one and the same thing in two aspects; and Catholicism, the principle of the universal Christian Society, is also Romanism: that is, rests upon Rome as the origin and type of universality, manifesting itself in a mystic dualism

---

¹ Bianchi, lib. i. cap. iv.

which corresponds to the two natures of its Founder. As Divine and eternal, its head is the Pope, to whom all souls have been entrusted; as human and temporal, the Emperor, commissioned to rule men's bodies and acts.'[1]

Mr. Bryce has here clearly seen the concrete unity of the Christian world; but he has missed the order which creates that unity. His description is what Boniface VIII. calls 'a monster with two heads.' Mr. Bryce quotes this saying in a note. If he had mastered the spiritual element as he has mastered the political, Mr. Bryce's book would have ranked very high among great authors.

Mr. Freeman, in an article on Mr. Bryce's book, is nearer to the true conception. He writes as follows:

'The theory of the Mediæval Empire is that of an universal Christian Monarchy. The Roman Empire and the Catholic Church are two aspects of one Society.' . . . 'At the head of this Society, in its temporal character as an Empire, stands the temporal chief of Christendom, the Roman Cæsar; at its head, in its spiritual character as a Church, stands the spiritual chief of Christendom, the Roman Pontiff. Cæsar and Pontiff alike rule by Divine right.'[2]

Now here are two things to be noted. First, that the Emperor holds an office of human creation; the Pontiff an office of Divine creation. Secondly, that the office of Divine creation is for a higher end than the office which is of human origin. The former is for the eternal, the latter for the earthly happiness of man.

But, as I have said before, the office of Divine cre-

---

[1] *The Holy Roman Empire*, p. 108. (Macmillan, 1871.)
[2] Freeman's *Historical Essays*, pp. 136–137. (Macmillan, 1872.)

ation, ordained to guide men to an eternal end, is higher than the office of human origin, directed to an earthly and temporal end; and in this the perfect unity and subordination of the whole is constituted and preserved.

Nevertheless, both Mr. Bryce and Mr. Freeman bring out clearly what Boniface means when he says that the two swords are *in Ecclesia*, in the Church, and *in potestate Ecclesiæ, in the power* of the Church.

To this I may add the following passage from the late Cardinal Tarquini,[1] who states the whole subject with great precision:—

'The Civil Society of Catholics is distinguished from others by this—that it consists of the same assemblage of men as the Church of Christ, that is, the Catholic Church, consists of: so that it in no way constitutes a real body diverse and separate from the Church; but both (societies) together have the character of a twofold federative association and obligation inhering in the same multitude of men, whereby the Civil Society under the government of the Civil Magistrate exerts its powers to secure the temporal happiness of men, and, under the government of the Church, to secure eternal life; and in such wise that eternal life be acknowledged to be the last and supreme end to which temporal happiness and the whole temporal life is subordinate; because if any man do not acknowledge this, he neither belongs to the Catholic Church, nor may call himself Catholic. Such, then, is the true notion of the Civil Society of Catholics. It is a society of men who so pursue the happiness of this life as thereby to show that it ought to be subordinate to the attainment of eternal happiness,

---

[1] Tarquini, *Juris Eccl. Publici Institutiones*, p. 56. (Rome, 1873.)

which they believe can be attained alone under the direction of the Catholic Church.'

We have here the full and genuine doctrine of the *Unam Sanctam*—the one body, the two swords, the subordination of the material to the spiritual sword, the indirect power of the spiritual over the temporal whensoever it deviates from the eternal end.

Dr. Döllinger's interpretation, then, is strictly correct—namely, ' It was therefore,' he says, ' the indirect power of the Church over the temporal power of Kings which the Pope defended in these Bulls;' but that power of the Pope is itself Spiritual.

VII. From this doctrine Cardinal Tarquini draws the following conclusions:

1. In things temporal, and in respect to the temporal end (of Government), the Church has no power in Civil society.

The proof of this proposition is that all things merely temporal are (*præter finem Ecclesiæ*) beside, or outside of, the end of the Church. It is a general rule that no society has power in those things which are out of its own proper end.

2. In whatsoever things, whether essentially or by accident, the spiritual end, that is, the end of the Church, is necessarily involved, in those things, though they be temporal, the Church may by right exert its power, and the Civil State ought to yield.[1]

In these two propositions we have the full explana-

---
[1] Tarquini, *Juris Eccl. Publici Institutiones*, p. 57.

tion of the indirect spiritual power of the Church. I give it in Cardinal Tarquini's words—

'*Directly* the care of temporal happiness alone belongs to the State, but *indirectly* the office also of protecting morals and religion; so, however, that this be done dependently on the Church, forasmuch as the Church is a society to which the care of religion and morals is directly committed.

'That which in the Civil Society is indirect and dependent, is direct and independent in the Church; and, on the other hand, the end which is proper and direct to the Civil State, that is, temporal happiness, falls only *indirectly*, or so far as the spiritual end requires, under the power of the Church.

'The result of all this is—

'1. That the Civil Society, even though every member of it be Catholic, is not subject to the Church, but plainly independent in temporal things which regard its temporal end.

'2. That the language of the Fathers, which seems to affirm[1] an absolute independence of the Civil State, is to be brought within this limit.'

VIII. I will now give a summary of this matter in the words of Suarez, and also his comment on the terminology used by Canonists and theologians on this subject.

He says that the opinion which gives to the Pontiff *direct temporal* power over all the world is false.

Next, he sets aside the opinion that the Pontiff has this direct temporal power over the Church.

He then gives as the true opinion that which has been affirmed—namely, that the Pontiff has not *direct*

---

[1] Tarquini, *Juris Eccl. Publici Institutions*, p. 55 *and note*.

temporal power, except in those States of which he is Temporal Prince; but that he has a *spiritual* power *indirectly* over temporal things, in so far as they affect the salvation of men or involve sin.[1]

One chief cause of the confusion of Regalists and our non-Catholic adversaries has been the uncertain use of language, and the want of a fixed terminology until a certain date.

The word *Temporal* was used in two senses. It was used to signify the power of Civil Rulers in the order of nature. And in this sense the Church has never claimed it for its head. It was used also to signify the *spiritual* power of the Pontiff *when incident indirectly upon temporal things*. The spiritual power, then, had a temporal effect, and took, so to speak, its colour and name from that use, remaining always spiritual as before.

For instance, we speak of 'the Colonial power' of the Crown, meaning the Imperial power applied to the government of the Colonies; in like manner the Spiritual power of the Pope, applied indirectly to temporal things, was (*improprie*) improperly called Temporal, and this *usus loquendi* gave rise to much misinterpretation.

What I have here stated was the judgment of Bellarmine, who, in his answer to Barclay, writes as follows:—

'Barclay says that there are two opinions among Catholics (on the power of the Pontiff). The one, which most Canonists follow, affirms that in the Supreme Pontiff, as Vicar of

[1] Suarez, *De Legibus*, lib. iii. c. vi.

Christ, both powers, Spiritual and Temporal, exist: the other, which is the common opinion of Theologians, affirms that the power of the Supreme Pontiff, as Vicar of Christ, is strictly spiritual in itself; but that, nevertheless, he may, by the same, dispose temporal things so that they be ordered for spiritual ends.'[1]

Barclay argued that the power of the Pope in temporal things was a free and open opinion among Catholics: Bellarmine, in replying, says:—

'That this power is in the Pope is not opinion but certitude among Catholics, though there be many discussions as to *what* and *of what quality* the power is: that is to say, whether it be *properly* and *in itself* of a *temporal* kind, or whether it be not rather *spiritual*, but by a certain necessary consequence, and in order to spiritual ends, it dispose of temporal things.'[2]

Bellarmine states his own opinion in these words:

'Temporal Princes, when they come to the family of Christ, lose neither their princely power nor jurisdiction; but they become subject to him whom Christ has set over His family, to be governed and directed by him in those things which lead to eternal life.'[3]

Now, from these passages it would appear that in Bellarmine's judgment the opinions of the Canonists and the Theologians practically came to one and the same thing, though their language was different. By Temporal Power some earlier Canonists may perhaps have intended a power temporal in itself; but the later Canonists did not intend more than a Spiritual power

---

[1] Bellarmine, *De Potestate Summi Pontificis*, cap. i. p. 848 A, Cologne, 1617.
[2] *Ibid.* cap. iii. p. 852 A.   [3] *Ibid.* cap. iii. p. 858 A.

over temporal things: which the Theologians also asserted. But this use of the word *temporal* seemed to imply that the *quality* of the power was not *spiritual*, as the Theologians asserted. This ambiguity is the source of the misunderstandings which we daily read in attacks upon the Catholic Church. I can the more readily believe the good faith of those who so misconceive it, because I can remember that I was misled by the same mistake for many years. For instance, the Canonists affirm that the whole world is the territory of the Pontiff (*Territorium Pontificis*). But they do so in answering the objection, that where the Pontiff acts spiritually in the territory of any temporal Prince, he is invading the territory of another. The meaning is evident: namely, that the Pontiff has universal jurisdiction over the whole world. But this does not say that his jurisdiction is temporal. It affirms only that it runs into all the world. It merely affirms that it is universal: and the same writers assert that in itself it is only Spiritual.[1]

We have been told that Bellarmine's book was put upon the Index. But, after a judicial examination, it was removed by order of the Holy See, and its perfect soundness acknowledged.

Suarez lays down precisely the same doctrine as Bellarmine. He says:—

'Those authors who teach absolutely that the Pope has Supreme Power, and that *temporal*, in the whole world, mean this, "that the Pontiff, in virtue of his *Spiritual* Power and jurisdiction, is superior to Kings and temporal Princes, so as to

[1] Tarquini, p. 46.

direct them in the use of their *temporal* Power in order to *Spiritual* ends."'

He then goes on :—

' For though they sometimes speak indistinctly, and without sufficient clearness, or even (*improprie*) incorrectly—because the power of the Pope is not temporal but spiritual, which contains under itself things temporal, and is exercised about them *indirectly*, that is, for the sake of Spiritual things—nevertheless they often make this sense clear, and lay down their distinctions either expressly or virtually; for they affirm that the Pontiff can do some things *indirectly*, but deny that he can do them *directly*.'[1]

But if the Pope had *temporal* power properly so called, he could do all things *directly*. This negative proves that the power of which they spoke was only Spiritual.

Suarez further says :—

' Subjection is of two kinds—direct and indirect. Subjection is called *direct* when it is within the end and limits of the same power; it is called *indirect* when it springs from direction to a higher end, which belongs to a higher and more excellent power. The proper Civil Power in itself is directly ordained for the fitting state and temporal happiness of the human commonwealth in time of this present life; and therefore the power itself is called temporal. The Civil Power, therefore, is then called supreme in its own order when within the same, and in respect to its end, the ultimate resolution (of power) is made within its own sphere.' . . . ' The chief ruler is, then, subordinate to no superior in order to the same end of

---

[1] Suarez, *Defensio Fidei Catholicæ*, tom. xxiv. lib. iii. c. xxii. 2nd ed. Paris, 1869.

Civil Government. But, as temporal and civil happiness are related to that which is spiritual and eternal, it may happen that the matter of Civil Government must be otherwise ordered and directed, in order to spiritual welfare, than the Civil policy alone seems to require. And then, though the temporal Prince and his power do not directly depend in their acts upon any other power in the same (*i. e.* the temporal) order, which also regards the same end only, nevertheless it may happen that it needs to be directed, helped, and corrected in the matter of its government by a superior power, which governs men in order to a more excellent and eternal end; and then this dependence is called *indirect*, because that higher power is not exercised in respect to temporal things (*per se*) of its own nature, nor for its own sake, but indirectly, and for another end.'[1]

It will be seen here :—
1. That the superior power cannot be temporal, or its jurisdiction would be direct.
2. That, if temporal, it would not be of a *higher*, but of the *same order*.
3. That, therefore, the claim of indirect power is an express exclusion of temporal power, properly so called, from the spiritual supremacy of the Head of the Church.

Suarez states, but rejects, the opinion of certain early Canonists and Jurists who taught that the power of the Pontiff over any temporal thing was also temporal in itself. He then states and proves that this indirect power is *Spiritual* only. After speaking of the power of the Keys, he says :—

'In no other place did Christ imply that He gave to Peter

[1] Suarez, *Defensio Fidei, &c.* lib. iii. cap. v. sect. 2.

or to the Church temporal dominion, or a proper and direct royalty; nor does Ecclesiastical tradition show this, but rather the reverse.'[1]

With these authorities before us, there can be little difficulty in explaining the texts usually quoted by adversaries, who desire to fasten on the *Unam Sanctam* and upon the Catholic Church a claim to temporal power, that is, temporal in its root and in itself.

The passages usually quoted from Pope Nicholas, St. Bernard, St. Thomas, Alvarez, Hugo of St. Victor, St. Bonaventura, Durandus, and others, are fully discussed and proved by Bellarmine to affirm no more than Spiritual power; and that indirectly over temporal matters, when they involve the Spiritual end of the Church.[2]

IX. I hope sufficiently to prove hereafter what I asserted—namely, that though a supreme spiritual authority be inherent in the Divine constitution and commission of the Church, its exercise in the world depends on certain moral and material conditions, by which alone its exercise is rendered possible or just. This shall be shown by treating the subjects raised by the 'Expostulation;'[3] namely, the deposing power, and the use of political force or penal legislation in matters of religion. I hope, and I believe, that I am able to show that the moral condition of the Christian world made justifiable in other ages that which would be un-

---

[1] Suarez, *Defensio Fidei, &c.* lib. iii. cap. v. sect. 14.
[2] This may be seen in his *Controversia de Summo Pontifice*, cap. v.; and in Bianchi's work, *Della Potestà*, tom. i. p. 91, lib. i. ch. x. xi.
[3] *Expostulation*, p. 26.

justifiable in this; and that the attempt to raise prejudice, suspicion, and hostility against the Catholic Church at this day and in England by these topics, is an act essentially unjust; from which a real science of history ought to have preserved Mr. Gladstone. I must repeat here again that between the Vatican Council and these subjects there is no more relation than between jurisprudence and the equinox. Some fifteen Councils of the Church, of which two are General, have indeed recognised and acted upon the supremacy of the Spiritual authority of the Church over temporal things; but the Infallibility of the Roman Pontiff is one thing, his supreme judicial authority is another. And the Definition of Infallibility by the Vatican Council has in no way, by so much as a jot or tittle, changed or affected that which was infallibly fixed and declared before. But, as I will go on to show, even infallible laws cease to apply when the subject matter is wanting, and the necessary moral conditions are passed away.

I must acknowledge, therefore, that the following words fill me with surprise. Speaking of Dr. Doyle and others, he says:—

'Answers in abundance were obtained, tending to show that the doctrines of deposition and persecution, of keeping no faith with heretics, and of universal dominion, were obsolete beyond revival.'[1]

This passage implicitly affirms what I hope explicitly to prove. How can laws become *obsolete*, but by the cessation of the moral conditions which require or

[1] *Expostulation*, p. 26.

justify their exercise? How can laws, the exercise of which is required by the permanent presence of the same moral conditions which called them into existence, become obsolete? I pass over the 'no faith with heretics,' which is an example of the injustice which pervades the Pamphlet. I should have thought it impossible for Mr. Gladstone not to know the true meaning of this controversial distortion: but I am willing to believe that he did not know it; for if he had, it would have been impossible for such as he is to write it.

The moral principles on which the exercise of supreme powers and rights was justifiable in the age of Boniface VIII. exist no longer in the nineteenth century in England. Let no one cynically pretend that this is to give up or to explain away. I read the other day these words:—

'The Pope has sent forth his prohibitions and his anathemas to the world, and the world has disregarded them. The faithful receive them with conventional respect, and then hasten to assure their Protestant friends that Papal edicts can make no possible difference in the conduct of any human being.'[1]

Nothing can be less true. The first principles of morals forbid the exercise of the supreme judicial power of the Church on such a civil order as that of England. When it was *de facto* subject to the Church, England had by its own free will accepted the laws of Christendom. It can never be again subject to such laws except on the same condition—namely, by its

[1] *Times*, Wednesday, December 30, 1874, in leading article on the Pope.

own free will. Till then the highest laws of morality render the exercises of such Pontifical acts in England impossible.

Mr. Gladstone has called on Pius IX. to repudiate such powers.[1] But Pius IX. cannot repudiate powers which his predecessors justly exercised, without implying that their actions were unjust. He need not repudiate them for himself, for the exercise of them is impossible, and, if physically possible, would be morally impossible, as repugnant to all equity, and, under correction, I will say to natural justice. The infallible witness for justice, and equity, and charity among men, cannot violate these laws which unerringly govern his office.

X. The command of our Lord to the Apostles: 'Go ye into the whole world and preach the Gospel to every creature: he that believeth and is baptised shall be saved, but he that believeth not shall be condemned'[2]—clearly invests the Church with the authority to baptise every creature. But the exercise of this right was suspended upon a moral condition. It conveyed no right to baptise any man against his will; nor without an act of faith on his part. But an act of faith is a spontaneous and voluntary act of submission, both of intellect and will, to the truth, and to the teacher who delivers it. The absolute and universal authority therefore of the Church to baptise depends upon the free and voluntary act of those who believe, and, through their own spontaneous submission, are willing to be baptised.

---

[1] *Expostulation*, p. 26.   [2] St. Mark xvi. 15, 16.

The Church so regards the moral conditions on which its acts depend, that as a rule it will not even suffer an infant to be baptised unless at least one of the parents consents.

In like manner the power of absolution, which has no limit of time or of subject, can be exercised only upon those who are willing. Confession and contrition, both voluntary acts of the penitent, are absolutely necessary to the exercise of the power of the Keys.

This principle will solve many questions in respect to the Spiritual authority of the Church over the Civil State.

First, it shows that, until a Christian world and Christian Rulers existed, there was no subject for the exercise of this spiritual authority of judgment and correction. Those who amuse themselves by asking why St. Peter did not depose Nero, will do well to find out whether people are laughing with them or at them. Such questions are useful. They compendiously show that the questioner does not understand the first principles of his subject. If he will find out why St. Peter neither baptised nor absolved Nero, he will have found out why he did not depose him. Until a Christian world existed there was no *apta materia* for the supreme judicial power of the Church in temporal things. Therefore St. Paul laid down as a rule of law that he had nothing to do in judging those that were without the unity of the Church.

But when a Christian world came into existence, the Civil society of man became subject to the Spiritual direction of the Church. So long, however, as individuals only subjected themselves, one by one, to its authority, the conditions necessary for the exercise of its office were not fully present. The Church guided men, one by one, to their eternal end; but as yet the collective society of nations was not subject to its guidance. It is only when nations and kingdoms become socially subject to the supreme doctrinal and judicial authority of the Church that the conditions of its exercise are verified. When the senate and people of the Roman Empire were only half Christian, the Church still refrained from acts which would have affected the whole body of the State. When the whole had become Christian, the whole became subject to the Divine Law, of which the Roman Pontiff was the supreme expositor and executive.

It would be endless to state examples in detail. I will take, therefore, only one in which the indirect spiritual power of the Church over the temporal State is abundantly shown. Take, for instance, the whole subject of Christian Matrimony: the introduction of the Christian law of the unity and indissolubility and sacramental character of marriage; the tables of consanguinity and of affinity; the jurisdiction of the Church over matrimonial cases. This action of the Pontifical law upon the Imperial law, and the gradual conformity of the Empire to the Church, exhibits in a clear and complete way what is the power claimed by the Church over the temporal laws of Princes.

The Council of Trent reserves matrimonial causes to the Ecclesiastical Tribunals; and in the Syllabus the proposition is condemned that they belong to the Civil jurisdiction.[1]

[1] Sess. xxiv. De Ref. can. xii.

In like manner, in prohibiting duels, the Council declares temporal penalties against not only the principals, but those also who are guilty of permitting them.¹

In like manner, again, the Christian law of faith and morals passed into the public law of Christendom. Then arose the Christian jurisprudence, in which the Roman Pontiff was recognized as the supreme Judge of Princes and of People, with a twofold coercion: spiritual by his own authority, and temporal by the secular arm. These two acted as one. Excommunication and deposition were so united in the jurisprudence of Christendom, that he who pronounced the sentence of excommunication pronounced also the sentence of deposition; as before the repeal of our Test Acts, if a member of the Church of England became Catholic, or even Nonconformist, he was *ipso facto* incapable of sitting in Parliament or holding office of State. And by the first of William III. the heir to the Crown, if he become Catholic, or marry a Catholic, *ipso facto* forfeits the succession. Nothing is more certain upon the face of history, and no one has proved more abundantly than Dr. Döllinger, that in every case of deposition, as of Philip le Bel, Henry IV. of Germany, Frederic II., and the like, the sentence of the Electors, Princes, States, and people, and the public opinion and voice of nations, had already pronounced sentence of rejection upon those tyrants before the Pontiffs pronounced the sentence of excommunication and deposition. It was only by the faith and free will of nations that they became socially subject to

---

¹ Sess. xxv. cap. xix.

this jurisprudence; it was by their free will that it was maintained in vigour; and it was in conformity with their free will that it was exercised by the Pontiffs. Their free sentence preceded the Pontifical sentence. It was at their prayer, and in their behalf, that it was pronounced. The moral condition of spontaneous acceptance, and the material conditions of execution, were alike present, rendering these supreme Pontifical acts legitimate, right, lawful, wise, and salutary.

XI. And here I shall be met with the answer: 'You justify, then, the deposition of princes, and therefore you hold that the Pope may depose Queen Victoria.' Such, I am sorry to say, is the argument of the 'Expostulation;' for if it be not, why was it implied? I altogether deny the argument, or inference, or call it what you will. I affirm that the deposition of Henry IV. and Frederic II. of Germany were legitimate, right, and lawful; and I affirm that a deposition of Queen Victoria would not be legitimate, nor right, nor lawful, because the moral conditions which were present to justify the deposition of the Emperors of Germany are absent in the case of Queen Victoria; and therefore such an act could not be done.

This is not a mere personal opinion of my own, or even a mere opinion of theologians. What I have affirmed has been declared by the authority of Pius VI. In a letter from the Congregation of Cardinals of the College of Propaganda, by order of His Holiness Pius VI., addressed to the Roman Catholic Archbishops of Ireland, dated Rome, June 23, 1791, we read as follows:—

'In this controversy a most accurate discrimination should be made between the genuine rights of the Apostolical See and those that are imputed to it by innovators of this age for the purpose of calumniating. The See of Rome never taught that faith is not to be kept with the heterodox—that an oath to kings separated from Catholic communion can be violated—that it is lawful for the Bishops of Rome to invade their temporal rights and dominions. We, too, consider an attempt or design against the life of kings and princes, even under the pretext of religion, as a horrid and detestable crime.'

I may add that this passage was not unknown to Dr. Döllinger, who quotes it at p. 51 in his work on 'The Church and the Churches.'

But lest any one should reply that this was said when Catholics were under penal laws, and with a view to blinding the English Government, I will add that no one has more frankly and forcibly expressed this than Pius IX., in the very text of which Mr. Gladstone has quoted a part. The Holy Father, on July 20, 1871, thus addressed a Literary Society in Rome:—

'In the variety of subjects which will present themselves to you, one appears to me of great importance at this time; and that is, to defeat the endeavours which are now directed to falsify the idea of the Infallibility of the Pope. Among all other errors, that is malicious above all which would attribute (to the Infallibility of the Pope) the right of deposing sovereigns, and of absolving people from the obligation of allegiance.

'This right, without doubt, has been exercised by the Supreme Pontiffs from time to time in extreme cases, but it has nothing to do with the Pontifical Infallibility; neither does it flow from the Infallibility, but from the authority of the Pontiff.

'Moreover, the exercise of this right in those ages of faith which respected in the Pope that which he is, that is to say, the Supreme Judge of Christendom, and recognised the benefit of his tribunal in the great contentions of peoples and of sovereigns, was freely extended (by aid, as was just, of public jurisprudence, and the common consent of nations) to the gravest interests of States and of their rulers.'

So far Mr. Gladstone quoted from what was before him. Unfortunately, he appears not to have known what followed. Pius IX. went on to say:—

'But altogether different are the conditions of the present time from the conditions (of those ages); and malice alone can confound things so diverse, that is to say, the infallible judgment in respect to truths of Divine Revelation with the right which the Popes exercised in virtue of their authority when the common good demanded it. They know better than we, and everybody can discern the reason why such an absurd confusion of ideas is stirred up at this time, and *why hypothetical cases are paraded of which no man thinks*. It is because every pretext, even the most frivolous and furthest from the truth, is eagerly caught at, provided it be of a kind to give us annoyance, and to excite civil rulers against the Church.

'Some would have me interpret and explain even more fully the Definition of the Council.

'I will not do it. It is clear in itself, and has no need of other comments and explanations. Whosoever reads that Decree with a dispassionate mind has its true sense easily and obviously before him.'[1]

Discorsi di Pio Nono, July 20, 1871, p. 203, Rome, 1872.

Now, the Holy Father in these words has abundantly shown two things: first, that they who connect Infallibility with the Deposing Power are talking of what they do not understand; and, secondly, that the moral conditions which justified and demanded the deposition of tyrannical Princes, when the mediæval world was both Christian and Catholic, have absolutely ceased to exist, now that the world has ceased to be Catholic, and has ceased to be even Christian. It has withdrawn itself socially as a whole, and in the public life of nations, from the unity and the jurisdiction of the Christian Church. In this it differs altogether from the mediæval world. And it differs also from the ancient world. For, the ancient world had never yet believed the faith; the modern world has believed, but fallen from its faith. The ancient world was without the unity of the Christian Church *de facto et de jure*. The modern world is without *de facto;* and this has changed all the moral conditions of the subject. The Church never, indeed, loses its jurisdiction *in radice* over the baptised, because the character of baptism is indelible; but unless the moral conditions justifying its exercise be present, it never puts it forth. As Mr. Gladstone has cited the example of Queen Elizabeth, implying that he sees no difference between Queen Elizabeth and Queen Victoria, I will add that Queen Elizabeth was baptised a Catholic; that she was crowned as a Catholic; that she received Holy Communion in the High Mass of her consecration as a Catholic; that she was both *de jure* and *de facto* a subject of the Catholic Church; that the majority of the people of England were still Catholic.

What one of all these conditions is present in the case which I refuse to put in parallel? The English Monarchy has been withdrawn for three centuries from the Catholic Church; the English people are wholly separate; the Legislation of England has effaced every trace of the jurisprudence which rendered the Pontifical acts of St. Gregory VII. and Innocent IV. legitimate, just, and right. The public laws of England explicitly reject and exclude the first principles of that ancient Christian and Catholic jurisprudence. Not only is every moral condition which could justify such an act absent, but every moral condition which would render such an act unjustifiable, as it would seem to me, is present.[1] This is a treatment of history which is not scientific, but shallow; and a dangerous use of inflammatory rhetoric, when every calm dictate of prudence and of justice ought to forbid its indulgence. 'The historic spirit,'[2] commended in the ' Expostulation,' would have led to such a treatment of this question as Mr. Freeman wisely recommends.

'The cause of all this diversity and controversy—a diversity and controversy most fatal to historic truth—is to be traced to the unhappy mistake of looking at the men of the twelfth century with the eyes of the nineteenth; and still more of hoping to extract something from the events of the twelfth century to do service in the controversies of the nineteenth.'[3]

XII. For the same reasons I deplore the haste, I must say the passion, which carried away so large a

---

[1] Appendix B.   [2] *Expostulation*, p. 14.
[3] Freeman's *Historical Essays*, ' St. Thomas of Canterbury and his Biographers,' p. 80.

mind to affirm or to imply that the Church at this day would, if she could, use torture, and force and coercion, in matters of religious belief. I am well aware that men of a mind and calibre as far removed from Mr. Gladstone as almost to constitute a different species, have at times endeavoured to raise suspicion and animosity against Catholics, by affirming that if they became the majority in this country—a danger certainly not proximate—they would use their power to compel men to conform to the Catholic faith. In the year 1830 the Catholics of Belgium were in a vast majority, but they did not use their political power to constrain the faith or conscience of any man. The ' Four Liberties ' of Belgium were the work of Catholics. This is the most recent example of what Catholics would do if they were in possession of power. But there is one more ancient and more homely for us Englishmen. It is found at a date when the old traditions of the Catholic Church were still vigorous in the minds of men. It will therefore show that in this at least we owe nothing to modern progress, nor to the indifference of Liberalism. If the modern spirit had any share in producing the Constitution in Belgium, it certainly had no share in producing the Constitution of Maryland. Lord Baltimore, who had been Secretary of State under James I., in 1633, emigrated to the American Plantations, where, through Lord Strafford's influence, he had obtained a grant of land. He was accompanied by men of all minds, who agreed chiefly in the one desire to leave behind them the miserable religious conflicts which then tormented England. They named their new country Maryland, and there they settled. The oath of the Governor was in these terms: 'I will not, by myself or any other, directly or indirectly, molest any person professing to believe in Jesus Christ, for or in respect of religion.' Lord Baltimore invited the Puritans of Massachusetts, who, like himself, had renounced their country for conscience' sake, to come into Maryland. In 1649, when active persecution had sprung up again in England, the Council of Maryland, on the 21st of April, passed this Statute: 'And whereas the forcing of the conscience in matters of religion hath frequently fallen out to be of dangerous consequence in the Commonwealth where it has been practised, and for the more quiet and peaceable government of the Province, and the better to preserve mutual love and amity among the inhabitants, no person within the Province professing to believe in Jesus Christ shall be anyways troubled, molested, or discountenanced for his or her religion, or in the free exercise thereof.'[1] The Episcopalians and Protestants fled from Virginia into Maryland. Such was the Commonwealth founded by a Catholic upon the broad moral law I have here laid down—that faith is an act of the will, and that to force men to profess what they do not believe is contrary to the law of God, and that to generate faith by force is morally impossible. It was by conviction of the reason and by persuasion of the will that the world-wide unity of faith and communion were slowly built up among the nations. When once shattered, nothing but conviction and persuasion can restore it. Lord Baltimore was sur-

---

[1] Bancroft's *History of the United States*, vol. i. pp. 233, 235, 255, etc.

rounded by a multitude scattered by the great wreck of the Tudor persecutions. He knew that God alone could build them up again into unity; but that the equity of charity might enable them to protect and to help each other, and to promote the common weal.

I cannot refrain from continuing the history. The Puritan Commonwealth in England brought on a Puritan revolution in Maryland. They acknowledged Cromwell, and disfranchised the whole Catholic population. 'Liberty of conscience' was declared, but to the exclusion of 'Popery, Prelacy, and licentiousness of opinion.' Penal laws came of course. Quakers in Massachusetts, for the first offence, lost one ear; for the second, the other; for the third, had their tongue seared with a red-hot iron. Women were whipped, and men were hanged, for religion. If Catholics were in power to-morrow in England, not a penal law would be proposed, nor the shadow of constraint be put upon the faith of any man. We would that all men fully believed the truth; but a forced faith is a hypocrisy hateful to God and man. If Catholics were in power to-morrow, not only would there be no penal laws of constraint, but no penal laws of privation. If the Ionian Islands had elected, some years ago, to attach themselves to the Sovereignty of Pius IX., the status of the Greek Church separate from Catholic Unity would have been tolerated and respected. Their Churches, their public worship, their Clergy, and their religious rites would have been left free as before. They were found in possession, which was confirmed by the tradition of centuries; they had acquired Civil rights, which enter into the laws of political justice, and as such would have been protected from all molestation.[1]

I have drawn this out, because a question absolutely chimerical has been raised to disturb the confidence of the English people in their Catholic fellow-countrymen. And I have given the reason and the principle upon which, if the Catholics were to-morrow the 'Imperial race' in these Kingdoms, they would not use political power to molest the divided and hereditary religious state of our people. We should not shut one of their Churches, or Colleges, or Schools. They would have the same liberties we enjoy as a minority. I hope the Nonconformists of England are prepared to say the same. As we are in days when some are 'invited,' and some are 'expected,' and some are 'required' to speak out, I will ask my fellow-countrymen of all religious kinds to be as frank as I am.

XIII. I have now given, I hope, sufficient evidence to prove the assertion made in the second letter quoted at the outset of these pages; namely:—

'That the relations of the Catholic Church to the Civil Powers have been fixed immutably from the beginning, because

---

[1] Our older writers, such as Bellarmine and Suarez, when treating of this subject, had before their eyes a generation of men who all had been in the unity of the faith. Their separation therefore was formal and wilful. Their separation from the unity of the Church did not release the conscience from its jurisdiction. But if Bellarmine and Suarez were living at this day, they would have to treat of a question differing in all its moral conditions. What I have here laid down is founded upon the principles they taught, applied to our times. Cardinal Tarquini, in treating the same matter, has dealt with it as it has been treated here.—*Juris Eccl. Publ. Institutiones*, p. 78.

they arise out of the Divine constitution of the Church, and out of the civil society of the natural order.'

And we have also seen how far from the truth are the confident assertions put forward lately, that the Church ascribes to its head Supreme Temporal as well as Supreme Spiritual Power.'

Further, we have seen with what strange want of reflection and of depth the Pontifical acts of the old Catholic world are transferred *per saltum* to a world which has ceased, in its public life and laws, to be Catholic, I may almost say, to be even Christian.

Finally, I have shown, I hope, what are the relations of the Church to the Civil Powers of the world; and I have given evidence to prove that those relations have been fixed from the beginning by reason of the Divine constitution of the Church, and have been declared by Councils, not only before the Council of the Vatican, but before the Council of Trent; and, therefore, that to charge upon the Vatican Council a change in these relations is not only an assertion without proof, but an assertion contrary to historical fact.

[1] *Expostulation, &c.* p. 27.

CHAPTER III.

AGGRESSIONS OF THE CIVIL POWER.

Mr. Gladstone says :—

'It is the peculiarity of Roman theology that, by thrusting itself into the temporal domain, it naturally, and even necessarily, comes to be a frequent theme of political discussion. To quiet-minded Roman Catholics it must be a subject of infinite annoyance that their religion is on this ground more than any other the subject of criticism; more than any other the occasion of conflicts with the State and of civil disquietude. I feel sincerely how much hardship their case entails, but this hardship is brought upon them altogether by the conduct of the authorities of their own Church.'[1]

His pamphlet from beginning to end bristles with the same accusations against the Catholic Church. His whole argument might be entitled, 'Reasons to show that in all Conflicts the Christian Church is always in the wrong, and the Civil State always in the right;' or, 'On the outrageous Claims'[2] and 'Exorbitances of Papal Assumptions,'[3] contrasted with the Innocence and Infallibility of Civil States.' This seems to me to be history read upside down; and not history only, but also Christianity. I can hardly persuade myself that Mr. Gladstone would contend that even in the Constitutions of Clarendon[4] St. Thomas of Canterbury was

---

[1] *Vatican Decrees*, p. 9.   [2] *Ibid.* p. 11.   [3] *Ibid.* p. 25.
[4] Mr. Gladstone says, upon what evidence I do not know, 'The Constitutions of Clarendon, cursed from the Papal Throne, were the

the aggressor, and Henry II. was within the law; or that either the Pope or Archbishop Langton began the conflict with the 'Papal minion John;' or, again, that in the question of Investitures and Ecclesiastical Simony, the Emperors of Germany were on the side of law and justice, and St. Gregory VII. and Innocent III. were aggressors. And yet all this is necessary to his argument. If he is not prepared to maintain this, the whole foundation is gone. But I do not know how any man who believes in the Divine office of the Christian Church can maintain such a thesis. And I have always believed that Mr. Gladstone does so believe the Christian Church to have a Divine office, which, within some limit at least, is independent of all human authority.

But as the contention before us is not of the past so much as of the present, I will come to the facts of the days in which we live.

My third proposition, then, is, that any collisions now existing between the Catholic Church and the States of Europe have been brought on by changes, not on the part of the Church, much less of the Vatican Council, but on the part of the Civil Powers, and that by reason of a systematic conspiracy against the Holy

---

work of the English Bishops.* St. Thomas himself says that 'Richard de Luci and Jocelin de Balliol, the abettors of the Royal tyranny, were the fabricators of those heretical pravities.'† Herbert of Bosham, who was present at Clarendon, says that they were the work of 'certain nobles (*proceres*) or chief-men of the kingdom.'‡ The Bishops were indeed terrified into submitting to them, but the Constitutions were in no sense their work.

* *Vatican Decrees*, pp. 57, 58.   † *Ep. St. Thomæ*, tom. iii. p. 12, ed. Giles, 1845.
‡ *Vita St. Thomæ*, tom. vii. p. 115, ed. Giles.

See. No one will ascribe to the Vatican Council the Revolution in Italy, the seizure of Rome in 1848, the invasion of the Roman State in 1860, the attacks of Garibaldi against Rome, ending with Mentana. And yet there are people who ascribe to the Vatican Council the breach at the Porta Pia, and the entry of the Italians into Rome. Such reasoners are proof against history, chronology, and logic. If anybody will persist in saying that the two and twenty years of aggression against the Holy See, from 1848 to 1870, were caused by Pius IX., I must address myself to other men. That Pius IX. has been in collision with those who attacked him is true enough. So is every man who defends his own house. Who, I ask, began the fray? From the Siccardi laws down to the laws of the Guarantees, who was the aggressor? But where the Pope is concerned logic seems to fail even in reasonable men. The other day Prince Von Bismarck told the Catholics of the Reichstag that they were accomplices of Kulmann, and therefore, as he implied, his assassins. Moreover, he affirmed that the war of France against Prussia was forced on the French Emperor by the Pope and the Jesuits. How providentially, then, though altogether fortuitously, no doubt, had Prussia been for three years massing its munitions of war and putting France in the wrong by intrigues in Spain, and fables from Ems. Nevertheless, all these things are believed. Prince Von Bismarck has said them. But surely they belong to the Arabian Nights.

. Now, I have already shown that, before the Vatican Council assembled, there was an opposition systematically organised to resist it. It was begun by certain

Professors at Munich. The Munich Government lent itself as an agent to Dr. Döllinger, and endeavoured to draw the other Governments of Europe into a combined attempt to hinder or to intimidate the Council. And this was done on the plea that the Council would not be free. I well remember that at one time we were told in Rome, that if the Council persevered with the Definition of the Infallibility, the French troops would be withdrawn. That is to say, that the Garibaldians would be let in to make short work of the Definition. It was said that the presence of the French troops was an undue pressure on the freedom of the Council, and that their departure was essential to its true liberty. There was a grim irony amounting to humour in this solicitude for the liberty of the Council.

I will now trace out more fully the history of this conspiracy, in order to put beyond question my assertion that the plan of attack was prepared before the Council met, and that the Falck Laws are a deliberate change made by the Civil Power of Prussia. the status of the Catholic Church in Germany being still unchanged.

I will here ask leave to repeat what I stated two years ago :

'In the year 1869 it was already believed that the Bavarian Government, through Prince Hohenlohe, had begun a systematic agitation against the Council. It was known that he had addressed a circular note to the European Governments. But the text of that note was not, so far as I know, ever made public. I am able now to give the text in full. It affords abundant proof of the assertion here made, that a deliberate conspiracy against the Council was planned with great artifice and speciousness of matter and of language. Moreover, the date of this document shows how long before the opening of the Council this opposition was commenced. The Council was opened on December 8, 1869. Prince Hohenlohe's note is dated on the 9th of the April preceding, that is to say, about eight months before the Council began. It runs as follows:—

'"Monsieur,—It appears to be certain that the Council convoked by His Holiness Pope Pius IX. will meet in the month of December next. The number of prelates who will attend it from all parts of the world will be much greater than at any former Council. This fact alone will help to give to its decrees a great authority, such as belongs to an Œcumenical Council. Taking this circumstance into consideration, it appears to me indispensable for every government to give it their attention, and it is with this view that I am about to address to you some observations.

'"It is not probable that the Council will occupy itself only with doctrines appertaining to pure theology; there does not exist at this moment any problem of this nature which requires a conciliar solution. The only dogmatic thesis which Rome would wish to have decided by the Council, and which the Jesuits in Italy and Germany are now agitating, is the question of the Infallibility of the Pope. It is evident that this pretension, elevated into a dogma, would go far beyond the purely spiritual sphere, and would become a question eminently political, as raising the power of the Sovereign Pontiff, even in temporal matters, over all the princes and peoples of Christendom. This doctrine, therefore, is of such a nature as to arouse the attention of all those Governments who rule over Catholic subjects.

'"There is a circumstance which increases still more

the gravity of the situation. I learn that among the commissions delegated to prepare matter, which later on is to be submitted to the deliberations of the Council, there is one which is occupied only on mixed questions, affecting equally international law, politics, and canon law. All these preparations justify our believing that it is the fixed intention of the Holy See, or at least of a party at present powerful in Rome, to promulgate through the Council a series of decrees upon questions which are rather political than ecclesiastical. Add to this that the *Civiltà Cattolica*—a periodical conducted by the Jesuits, and bearing an official character through the brief of the Holy Father—has just demanded that the Council shall transform into conciliar decrees the condemnations of the Syllabus, published on December 8, 1864. Now, the articles of this encyclical being directed against principles which are the base of modern public life, such as we find it among all civilised nations, it follows that Governments are under the necessity of asking themselves if it is not their duty to invite the serious consideration both of the Bishops who are their subjects, and of the future Council, to the sad consequences of such a premeditated and systematic overturning of the present relations between Church and State. It cannot, indeed, be denied that it is a matter of urgency for Governments to combine, for the purpose of protesting, either through their agents in Rome, or in some other way, against all decisions which the Council may promulgate without the concurrence of the representatives of the secular power, in questions which are at the same time of a political and religious nature.

'" I thought that the initiative in so important a matter should be taken by one of the great Powers; but not having as yet received any communication on this subject, I have thought it necessary to seek for a mutual understanding which will protect our common interests, and that without delay, seeing that the interval between this time and the meeting of the Council is so short. I therefore desire you to submit this matter to the Government to which you are accredited, and to ascertain the views and intentions of the Court of * * * in respect to the course which it deems advisable to follow. You will submit, for the approbation of M. * * *, the question whether it would not be advisable to fix beforehand the measures to be taken, if not jointly, at least identically, in order to enlighten the Holy See as to the attitude which the Governments of the Continent will assume in reference to the Œcumenical Council; or whether conferences composed of representatives of the States concerned would not be considered as the best means to bring about an understanding between their Governments.

'" I authorise you to leave a copy of this despatch with the Minister for Foreign Affairs at * * * , if he desires it; and I wish you to inform me as early as possible of the manner in which this communication may be received.

'" I have the honour, etc.,

'" HOHENLOHE.

'" *Munich, April* 9, 1869."'

No one could fail to see that this Circular had not Prince Hohenlohe for its author. We shall hereafter trace it to its legitimate origin.

'The indiction of the Council was no sooner published than the well-known volume called *Janus* appeared. It was said to be the work of many hands, and of various nations—of two at least. The chief object of its animosity was Rome, and its detailed hostility was levelled against the Infallibility of the Roman Pontiff and the Syllabus. The book was elaborately acrimonious and extravagantly

insolent against Rome. Its avowed aim was to rouse the
Civil Governments against the Council. The Sovereign
Pontiff had, with great wisdom and justice, dealt with the
Governments of Europe on the ground chosen by themselves. They had renounced the Catholic relations of
union hitherto subsisting between the Civil and Spiritual
Powers. Pius IX. took them at their word. He convened
the Spiritual Legislature of the Church; he did not invite
those who have gloried in their separation from it. This,
again, sharpened the jealousy and suspicion of the Governments. At this time came forth certain publications—to
which I will not more explicitly refer—avowedly intended
to excite the Civil Powers to active opposition.

'About the month of September 1869, as I have already
said, a document containing five questions was proposed by
the Bavarian Government to the Theological Faculty at
Munich. No one could for a moment doubt by what hand
those interrogatories also were framed; they were intended
to elicit the answer, that the action of the Council, if it
were to define the Infallibility of the Roman Pontiff, would
be irreconcilable not only with Catholic doctrine, but with
the security of Civil Governments. In due time the answers
appeared, leaving no doubt that both the questions and
the replies were inspired by one mind, if not written by one
and the same hand.

'We have already seen that Prince Hohenlohe, President
of the Council and Minister of Foreign Affairs in Bavaria,
addressed a letter to the French and other Catholic Governments, calling on them to interfere and to prevent the
"fearful dangers" to which the Council would expose the
modern world. Next, the Spanish Minister, Olozaga, hoped
that the Council would not meet, or at least would "not
approve, sanction, or ratify the Syllabus, which is in contradiction with modern civilisation." . He then threatened

the Church with the hostility of a league formed by the Governments of France, Italy, Portugal, Spain, and Bavaria. An Italian infidel then took up the game, and proposed an Anti-Œcumenical Council to meet at Naples. A French infidel was invited, who promised that his soul should be present, and said: "It is an efficacious and noble idea to assemble a council of ideas to oppose to the council of dogmas. I accept it. On the one side is theocratic obstinacy, on the other the human mind. The human mind is a divine mind, its rays on the earth, its star is above. . . . If I cannot go to Naples, nevertheless I shall be there. My soul will be there. I cry, Courage! and I squeeze your hand." The reader will forgive my repeating this trash, which is here inserted only to show how the liberals and infidels of Europe rose up at the instigation of Dr. Döllinger to meet the coming Council.

'About the month of June, in 1869, another despatch had been addressed by Prince Hohenlohe to the other Governments, inviting them to make common cause against the Council. It was extensively believed to be inspired by Prussia, the policy of which was thought to be, to put in contrast the liberty accorded to its own Catholic subjects in respect of the Council with the pedantic meddling of the Bavarian Government. At this time General Menabrea, under the same inspiration, addressed a circular to his diplomatic agents, proposing to the Powers to prevent the assembling of the Council, on the ground of their not having been invited to it. It was supposed at that time that this policy also was secretly supported by Berlin. A joint despatch was sent by Prince Hohenlohe and the Italian Government to the French Government, urging the withdrawal of the French troops from Rome during the Council, *to insure its freedom of deliberation.*

These preparations to oppose the Council were made before it had assembled. It met on December 8, 1869. In the following January, Dr. Döllinger received the freedom of a German city, in reward for his attacks on the Holy See.

'When the well-known *postulatum* of the Bishops, asking that the definition of the Papal Infallibility should be proposed to the Council, was made public, Dr. Döllinger openly assailed it; and the French Minister of Foreign Affairs, Count Daru, addressed a letter to the Holy See with a view to prevent the definition. Rome was at that time full of rumours and threats that the protection of the French army would be withdrawn. I had personally an opportunity of knowing that these threats were not mere rumours.

'At the same moment, while France was attacking the definition of the Pope's Infallibility, the Protestant Chancellor of Austria, Count Von Beust, addressed himself to the Canons of the Schema published in the *Augsburg Gazette*, which he declared would "provoke deplorable conflicts between the Church and State." Every European Government from that time put a pressure more or less upon the Council to prevent the definition.

'The source of this opposition, then, was Munich. The chief agent, beyond all doubt, was one who in his earlier days had been greatly venerated in Germany and in England. Truth compels me to ascribe to Dr. Döllinger the initiative in this deplorable attempt to coerce the Holy See, and to overbear the liberty of the Bishops assembled in Council. Prince Hohenlohe is assuredly no theologian. The documents published by him came from another mind and hand. Such was the opposition before and during the Council.

'What I have hitherto said to prove the conspiracy of

certain European Governments, and the intrigues of the Old Catholics against the Council, both before the assembling and during its sessions, would not have been needed if the *Diary of the Council* by Professor Friedrich had sooner come into my hands. I have been feeling in the dark for proofs which he brings to light by a series of astounding confessions. I had always believed in the conspiracy; but I never knew how systematic and how self-confident it was. I had always known that the Gnostic vainglory of German scientific historians was its chief instigator; but I never before imagined the stupendous conceit or the malevolent pride of its professors. A critique of Professor Friedrich's Diary, by some strong German hand, has appeared lately in one of our journals, and I cannot refrain from giving certain passages in final confirmation of what I have said above.

'And first as to the Governments. Professor Friedrich puts into the mouth of a diplomatist the following words: "The means by which the greatest amount of influence might be brought to bear on the Council would be a determined and plain manifestation of the public opinion of Europe in favour of the minority. Clearly the *Curia* could not prevent this; and it would add strength and numbers to the opposition, by giving it the assurance that, if at the last moment it found itself obliged to protest and appeal to the nation, the Governments and all intelligent laymen would support it. This measure would also secure 'weak and doubtful Bishops'" (*Diary*, p. 184). On the 26th of December, 1869, Friedrich wrote, " That he was considered by many persons to be residing in Rome as the representative of an approaching schism, if the majority obtained the upper hand in the Council " (p. 41). He says in another place: "It would not be the first time in the history of the Church that a schism had broken out. Church history recounts many such, besides that of the Greeks" (p. 196). The critic of Professor Friedrich's book writes as follows: "The alliance between 'German science' and diplomacy was not productive of all the results which at first had been looked for. Friedrich expresses himself very bitterly on this point; nevertheless he endeavoured all the more to excite German science to fresh efforts." Under date of the 27th of March (p. 202) he writes: "The Governments are by degrees acting an almost ridiculous part towards the Council — first boasts; then embarrassment connected with meaningless threats; and at last the confession that the right time has passed by, and that the Curia has command of the situation. If German science had not saved its position, and been able to establish a firm opposition in the Council, even in contradiction to its own will, and kept it alive; and if our Lord God had not also set stupidity and ignorance on the side of the Curia and of the majority, the Governments would have been put to shame in the sight of the whole world. Prince Hohenlohe, in fact, is the only statesman possessed of a deeper insight in this question, and by degrees he has come to be looked upon as belonging to the minority."[1]

'Of all the foreign sources from which the English newspapers drew their inspiration, the chief perhaps was the *Augsburg Gazette*. This paper has many titles to special consideration. The infamous matter of Janus first appeared in it under the form of articles. During the Council it had in Rome at least one English contributor. Its letters on the Council have been translated into English, and published by a Protestant bookseller in a volume by Quirinus.'

A distinguished bishop of Germany, one of the mi-

[1] Preface to Vol. III. *Sermons on Ecclesiastical Subjects*, p. xxv. &c.

nority opposed to the definition, whose cause the *Augsburg Gazette* professed to serve, delivered at the time his judgment on Janus, and the letters on the Council.

'Bishop Von Ketteler of Mainz publicly protested against "the systematic dishonesty of the correspondent of the *Augsburg Gazette*." "It is a pure invention," he adds, "that the Bishops named in that journal declared that Döllinger represented, as to the substance of the question (of Infallibility), the opinions of a majority of the German Bishops." And this, he said, "is not an isolated error, but part of a system which consists in the daring attempt to publish false news, with the object of deceiving the German public, according to a plan concerted beforehand." . . . . " It will be necessary one day to expose in all their nakedness and abject mendacity the articles of the *Augsburg Gazette*. They will present a formidable and lasting testimony to the extent of injustice of which party-men, who affect the semblance of superior education, have been guilty against the church." Again, at a later date, the Bishop of Mainz found it necessary to address to his diocese another public protest against the inventions of the *Augsburg Gazette*. "The *Augsburg Gazette*," he says, "hardly ever pronounces my name without appending to it a falsehood." . . . "It would have been easy for us to prove that every Roman letter of the *Augsburg Gazette* contains gross perversions and untruths. Whoever is conversant with the state of things here, and reads these letters, cannot doubt an instant that these errors are voluntary, and are part of a concerted system designed to deceive the public. If time fails me to correct publicly this uninterrupted series of falsehoods, it is impossible for me to keep silence when an attempt is made with so much perfidy to misrepresent my own convictions."

'Again, Bishop Hefele, commenting on the Roman correspondents of the *Augsburg Gazette*, says: "It is evident that there are people not bishops, but having relations with the Council, who are not restrained by duty and conscience." We had reason to believe that the names of these people, both German and English, were well known to us.

'Now the testimony of the Bishop of Mainz, as to the falsehoods of these correspondents respecting Rome and Germany, I can confirm by my testimony as to their treatment of matters relating to Rome and England. I do not think there is a mention of my own name without, as the Bishop of Mainz says, the appendage of a falsehood. The whole tissue of the correspondence is false.'[1]

I have quoted all this to show the small chance the people of England had of knowing the truth as to the state and acts of the Council, and also how systematic was the opposition organised against it in Germany.

After the suspension of the Council, the action of this conspiracy, hitherto secret, became open. Dr. Von Döllinger and certain Professors openly rejected the Vatican Council, accusing it of innovation. They therefore either took, or were called by, the name of 'Old Catholics.' This schism has never been in one stay. Its development has had three progressive stages. At first the Old Catholics professed to hold by the Council of Trent, and to reject only the Council of the Vatican. As such they claimed to be recognised by the Prussian law. But next, at a meeting at Augsburg, a large infusion of German Rationalists compelled them to enlarge their comprehension, and

[1] *Petri Priv.* part iii. pp. 4–7.

to include those who rejected most of the doctrines of the Council of Trent.

Lastly, at Cologne and Bonn, they received the accession of Anglicans, American Episcopalians, Greeks, and various Protestants.

The Old Catholic schism, therefore, has lost its meaning and its character, and has become a body without distinctive creed. Dr. Von Döllinger, at Bonn, last September, declared (if the report be correct) that Old Catholics are not bound by the Council of Trent.

In the sphere of theology and religion the movement is already paralysed, and has no future; but in the sphere of politics it has a great power of mischief. I have already shown how the first acts of the diplomatic and political hostility to the Council began at Munich. There can be little doubt that it reached Berlin through the Circular of Prince Hohenlohe, the present German Ambassador at Paris. The Berlin Government supported the Old Catholic Professors who rejected the Vatican Decrees, on the plea that the Council of Trent was known to the law in Prussia, but that the Council of the Vatican was not known to it. It was *exlex*. Therefore the Government recognised the legal status of the Old Catholics who held to the Council of Trent. How they will still recognise them as Old Catholics, now that they have rejected the Council of Trent at Bonn, it is not so easy to say. However, Dr. Reinkens was consecrated Bishop by a Jansenist Prelate, and received from the Berlin Government both legal recognition and a good salary. We shall see hereafter that the Government would thereby try to tempt the Catholic Clergy to its friendship, and to use the 'Old Catholic' schism as a weapon against the Catholic Church. The 'Old Catholic' schism has an attraction for certain minds in which there is a strong hankering after the Catholic Church without the courage to suffer for the truth's sake. An attempt, we have been told, was made to set up an 'Old Catholic' Church in London, but it met with little encouragement.

There is not a doubt that the Berlin Government aims at changing all the Catholics in Germany into Old Catholics.

The Old Catholics, in their appeal to the Civil Power, are doing what the Arians did after the Council of Nicæa. They have been, and they will be, the instigators of persecution against the Catholic Church. But they are blindly doing God's will. When the Church has been purified, their place will know them no more.

To return to the politicians and diplomatists. What was believed as to the conspiracy at Munich before the Council met has since been confirmed by the letters of Count Arnim, which ascribe his own action to the instigation of Dr. Döllinger. The Berlin Correspondent of the *Daily Telegraph*,[1] after noticing the discrepancy between the despatch of Count Arnim, published by Prince Bismarck, and his 'Pro Memoria,' which appeared in the *Vienna Presse*—the first 'treating the dogma of Infallibility as a mere theological dissertation,' and the second, ' seeing in it an event that must overthrow Catholicism and the peace of Catholic States '—proceeds to explain the contradiction thus:—

[1] *Tablet Newspaper*, Oct. 31 1874, p. 546.

'When Prince Hohenlohe, as leader of Bavarian foreign affairs, sent his well-known Circular to different Powers, explaining the dangers of that dogma, the German Chancellor applied to Count Arnim, who answered that the Bavarian Minister exaggerated the danger, being influenced by Döllinger. After this answer was sent to Berlin, Count von Arnim went on his holidays, and in passing Munich visited Prince Hohenlohe. There they spoke about Infallibility, *and Prince Hohenlohe acknowledged that the Circular was written under Döllinger's inspiration.* The Prince asked the Count to visit Döllinger, which he did. Döllinger convincingly explained to Arnim the importance of the dogma; and, on his return, Arnim tried everything to prevent the result of the Council by repeatedly advising Prince Bismarck to interfere; so the change, in Arnim's opinion, must be traced to Döllinger.'

Before we enter upon the present conflict in Germany, so carelessly touched and dismissed by Mr. Gladstone, it is necessary to record the fact that, in the year 1849, the 15th Article of the German Constitution affirmed, that ' Every religious Society shall order and manage its own affairs independently, but shall remain subject to the general power of the State.' The Prussian Constitution also recognized this independence. Such was the law until 1872. Under this law the Catholics were loyal, peaceful, and of unimpeachable allegiance to the State. They served it in peace; they fought for it in war. They helped to found the Empire in their blood. Who made the change? The Government of Berlin. The laws of 1849 have been violated, and a series of laws, which I will hereafter describe, have been forced upon the Catholics of Prussia. The conflict was thus begun, not by the Catholics nor by the Church, but by the Civil Power. Prince Von Bismarck is so conscious of this fact, that he has spared no accusation, how wild soever, against the Catholics to disguise and to mask it. The laws resisted now by the Bishops and Catholics of Prussia are not the old laws of their country, but innovations, intolerable to conscience, newly introduced, and inflicted upon them by the fine and imprisonment of five Bishops and 1,400, it is even said 1,700, clergy. Surely the day is past when anyone believes that the Falck Laws were caused by the Vatican Council. The French war was scarcely ended when Prince Von Bismarck accused the Catholics of Germany of disloyalty and conspiracy against the Empire. They had not even had time to be disloyal or to conspire. The Catholic blood shed in the war was not yet dry. He said then, as he said the other day, that he had secret evidence. Not a particle has ever been produced. For a time Englishmen were perplexed. They did not know what to believe. They could not conceive that Prince Von Bismarck would make such charges without evidence; but, little by little, the truth has come out. The Old Catholic conspiracy has been laid open to the world. The manly and inflexible constancy of the Catholic Bishops, Priests, and people of Germany has roused the attention of Englishmen, and they have come to know that no body of men were more gladly loyal to the Prussian Government than the Catholics on the basis of the laws of their country from 1848 to 1872; that no change whatsoever, by a jot or tittle, was made on their part; that, on the part of Government, a new and elaborate legislation, anti-Catholic and intolerable to conscience, was introduced in 1872. The whole innovation was on the part of Government. The new laws excluded the Clergy from the schools; banished the religious orders; made Government consent necessary to the nomination of a Parish Priest; fined and imprisoned Bishops for the exercise of their Spiritual office; subjected to the State the education of the Clergy, even to the examination for orders; and established a final tribunal of Ecclesiastical appeal in Berlin. And yet men were found who had still the hardihood to say that the Church had begun the conflict. At last, Dr. Friedberg, Professor of Law at Leipsic, and one of the chief advisers of Government in its Ecclesiastical policy, let out the real cause. With an incautious candour he has told us the truth.

I will take the account of Dr. Friedberg's book, 'The German Empire and the Catholic Church,' from a pamphlet of the Bishop of Mayence, entitled, 'The New Prussian Bills on the Position of the Church in reference to the State.'[1]

Bishop Ketteler begins by asking, 'What could prompt the Liberal party to denounce as Ultramontane presumption, and as a surrender of the essential rights of the State, that which, in the years 1848–1850, it had acknowledged as the necessary "consequence of its own principles"?' (p. 9)

Bishop Ketteler answers, 'The true reason of the thorough systematic change of the Liberal party, as well as of all those measures aimed against the lawful

[1] A translation made in Germany has been published by Messrs. Burns & Oates, 17 Portman Street.

rights of the Church, is "the spiritual power of the Church based upon the foundation of freedom"' (p. 11).

He then quotes an Address of Dr. Friedberg, in which he says, 'The Doctrinaires will still tell us that the all-sufficient remedy of this is the separation of the Church from the State; but, on the contrary, under actual circumstances, this would be a very injurious measure, *for the Church has become too much united to the people.*'

He then shows that wherever the Church is free, as in the United States, it is powerful, because it is the Church of the people. 'What would be the consequence,' he asks, 'with us if the Church were freed from the control of the State?" 'On the contrary,' says Dr. Friedberg, 'as the whole question has become now *one of main force*, the State must go so far as to deprive the Church of her influence over the people, in order that its own power may be firmly established' (pp. 10, 11).

Dr. Newman, more than thirty years ago, said that Governments establish and endow Churches as people cut the wings of magpies, that they may hop upon the lawn and pick up worms. 'Liberals love a tame Church.'

I quote this in answer to those who have been taunting the German Bishops with complaining of persecution and of yet holding to their legal status: Pharaoh has taught all oppressors 'not to let the people go.'

'Our crime as endangering the State,' says Bishop Ketteler, ' consists in this—that wheresoever the people and the Church are free, the people turn to the Church, and not to the doctrines of the Liberal party' (p. 13).

'Here we have the whole undisguised truth. To separate the Christian people from the Church, to deprive it of freedom, to subjugate it by force to Liberal Statecraft and human wisdom, thus reducing it to a Liberal State-religion—this is the triumph of modern science and knowledge which Liberalism and its professors offer to the German people' (p. 14).

Bishop Ketteler then goes on to give Dr. Friedberg's argument: 'The Protestant Church is, at this day, *an essential political agent*—solely by its opposition to Catholicism.'

Dr. Von Holzendorff says of the Protestant Church, that 'it has no intellectual unity, because a short-sighted orthodoxy has sown and fostered indifference towards the Church; and also from the fact that the Protestant Church did not create a constitution suited to its own spirit. Who could count upon the High Consistory Court of Berlin outliving for a day the separation of the Church from the State? or that the fiercest party strife would not break it up into sects? But what an opportunity for the compact mass of the Catholic Church as opposed to these dismembered elements,' &c.¹ This lets in light.

Bishop Ketteler then sums up: 'These confessions of a pretended Liberal deserve notice.

'First, the Protestant Church is "an essential politi-

---

¹ *Year-Book of the German Empire.* By Dr. F. von Holzendorff, Leipzig, p. 473, 1872.

cal agent," and especially so by her opposition to Catholicism.

'Secondly, the Protestant Church cannot endure freedom and independence. "After separation from the State it would be 'dismembered.' The High Consistory of Berlin would scarcely survive a day."

'Thirdly, out of these dismembered elements an increase would fall to the Catholic Church. Principles truly Liberal. No longer shall the power of truth under the protection of equal freedom decide between the different creeds. In the hands of the Liberals the Protestant Church is to become a "political agent," "a tool of the State," to fight against Catholicism. Even liberty of conscience on the part of the people is to be destroyed to avert the danger of their turning to the Catholic Church.

'Lastly, Dr. Friedberg refused to separate the Church from the State, because it would be "a severity and an injustice," forsooth, to the Old Catholics. If the Church were set free, the Government would lose "an immediate support and a *co-operation so necessary* to the State for *the internal reform of the Church*."'

The Bishop then sums up as follows :—The Government has changed its relations to the Catholic Church, 'not because the Catholic Church is dangerous to the State, nor because it is hostile to the Empire, nor because it will overbear the State ; these are not the motives, though they are daily expressed in Parliament and in the press by the Liberal party, to show that the Catholic Church must be robbed of her liberty, but because the German people must be torn away by force from the Church ; and in order to attain this end, the

Protestant State Church and the "Old Catholics" are to be used as weapons to fight the Catholic Church, and to destroy it internally,' &c. (p. 17).

Such is the end and aim: now for the means. Dr. Friedberg says, 'One must first attempt to draw off the waters carefully, letting them flow into other channels, and conducting them into reservoirs; what remains will then be easily absorbed into the air' (p. 19). In other words, dry up the Church; draw from it all intellectual, moral, and spiritual influence over the people; paralyse the action of its Pastors; substitute Bureaus, Registrars, Professors, State Teachers, and State Officials; make its worship a State Ritualism, a ceremonial of subjective feelings, not of objective Truth. This done, religion will soon evaporate. The sum of all, Bishop Ketteler says, is that

'The State will regard the Church as a historical established institution, which may be very useful to the State by fulfilling its peculiar and necessary mission for the civilisation of the German people, but which, on the other hand, may become dangerous to the State, and has become so.

'For the first reason the Church shall be not only tolerated but also be authorised by the State. For the second reason, it is to be rendered harmless.

'This will dry up the stream, and the rest will evaporate.'

After this I think even an English Nonconformist would read the *Unam Sanctam* with new eyes.

Now, the proximate means of accomplishing this draining of the Pontine Marshes is 'the inward and outward release' of the Clergy from all dependence on powers 'outside our nation,' and 'strangers to our national consciousness ;' that is to say, a spiritual blockade against the Church throughout the world, or 'our German consciousness' against Christianity.

The inward release of the Clergy is to be effected 'through their education' (pp. 29, 30). Their education is to be as follows:—

1. Every Priest is to go through an examination at a German College.
2. He is to study Theology for three years in a German *State University*.

All independent seminaries and religious colleges for boys are interdicted.

3. He is finally to be examined in the presence of a Commissary of the Government.
4. The State has the superior direction of all instruction of the Clergy.
5. It fixes the method of their teaching.
6. It decides the qualification of their teachers.

The Bishop is to be, in all these relations, dependent on the State; the State forms the Catholic Clergy to its own fashion; and the Bishop has only to receive them and to give them cure of souls.

The Bishop of Mayence justly says: 'A Clergy inwardly deprived of faith, falling under the bondage of unbelief and the spirit of the times, would, no doubt, become the perfect ideal of national education' (pp. 35, 36).

Next for the 'outward release' of the Clergy.

First it means that the State will regulate the appointment and deposition, and the correctional discipline of the Clergy by local Civil authorities, and partly by a Supreme Royal court for Clerical affairs.

The Clergy are therefore perfectly released:
> First, from the jurisdiction of the Head of the Church.
>
> Secondly, from the jurisdiction of their own Bishops.

The effect of this release is:
> First, that any fit and worthy Priest may be kept out of the cure of souls and all spiritual offices by the veto of the State.
>
> Second, that any unfit or unworthy, any immoral or heretical, Priest may be supported in defiance of his Bishop, to the scandal of the Church and the perdition of Souls.

An unlimited veto is an unlimited right of patronage.

What kind of man will grow up out of the soil of State Universities, and under the sun of State Patronage?

What priest of fidelity to the Church and of personal dignity of character will sell or lend himself to such a despotism?

We have read lately a little too much of the 'pliancy and servility' and 'degradation' of the Catholic Episcopate. What is the ideal of a Bishop in those who assail the Vatican Council and sympathise with the Old Catholics? By these laws the Clergy and Bishops are *liberated* or released from the foreign oppression of Rome. The Pope cannot suspend one of them. But the Royal Court may depose them all. Is Dr. Reinkens, with his sixteen thousand thalers a year, under the Falck Laws, independent, high-minded, and manly? Is the Archbishop of Posen, in his prison, pliant, servile, and degraded? This seems to me to 'put light for darkness, and darkness for light.' It would be an anxious sign of our time and state if an inverted moral sense should grow upon us.

The Bishop of Mayence finally sums up this external release of their Clergy as follows:

> These laws amount to—
> 1. Separation of the Church in Germany from Rome.
> 2. Annihilation of the powers of the Bishops.
> 3. The breaking up of all authority and discipline over the Clergy and people.
> 4. Unlimited control of the State over the Clergy, and over religion.
> 5. Universal moral corruption of the whole Church.
> 6. Introduction and encouragement of every form of error contrary to faith and to Christianity among the teachers.
> 7. Loss of Christian faith among the people.

The Bishop then protests against these laws as—

'A violation of all Christian liberties, and of all Constitutional rights; as an attempt to force on the Catholic Church the Royal Supremacy of the Protestant Reformation; as a violation of the Divine constitution and authority of the Catholic Church; and, finally, as leading men back again into the Cæsarism of the Pagan world, in which the temporal and spiritual sovereignty were united in one person. The separation of the two powers which the Divine Founder of Christianity has introduced for the protection of the liberties of human life in faith, conscience and religion would be once more extinguished in Germany. It would then be easy to overthrow, one after another, the other safeguards of the freedom of the people. The army, the official State press, or State school, or State Church, all united together would transplant the old despotism of the Pagans to German soil' (p. 49).

He concludes in these words:—

'Finally, these laws are in their whole substance revolutionary, and a denial of the historical positive development of the rights, and an uprooting of all the constitutional privileges, of the people. They will bring about a conflict with the Catholic Church, with its essential constitution and its doctrines; they attempt to force upon the Catholic Church a constitution similar to that of the Protestant Church. By placing all earthly power in the hands of one man they introduce the system of the heathen despotism into Germany.

'May God guard our German Fatherland from the disastrous consequences of such laws.'

Before this noble protest was published these Bills became law. I hope no Englishman will now say that the conflict in Germany was brought on by the Church. The pretext of Vatican Council is as transparently false as the plea of the wolf against the lamb. Such, then, are the Falck Laws; and I have read no part of Mr. Gladstone's 'Expostulation' with more sadness than the following words:—

'I am not competent to give any opinion upon the particulars of that struggle. The institutions of Germany, and the relative estimate of State power and individual freedom, are materially different from ours.'[1]

Are faith and conscience 'institutions' to be 'estimated' 'relatively'? Is religious freedom, to the vindication of which Mr. Gladstone has given a long public life, a matter to be measured by geogra-

[1] *The Vatican Decrees, &c.* p. 48.

phical or political conditions? I do not recognise this voice.

It may, I think, with safety be affirmed, that in the lamentable conflict now waging in Germany, the Berlin Government, urged on by the conspiracy of the 'Old Catholics,' aided, no doubt, at a later stage, by the pseudo-Liberals of Prussia, has been the aggressor.

The same could be abundantly proved in respect to the persecution of the Church in Switzerland. I have before me full and authentic evidence of the aggression of the Cantonal Governments of Bâle, Soleure, and Berne and others. But I will not prolong this chapter by a recital. The proof will be found in the Appendix C.

It would be as easy also to show that in Brazil the Government was the aggressor. The Bishop of Olinda is at this moment in penal servitude, for refusing religious rites at the burial of an excommunicated person.

This will, I hope, be deemed a sufficient proof of my third proposition, which in sum is this, that the present collisions between the Civil and Spiritual Powers have not been caused by the Church. There is everywhere a party aiming at the subversion of Christianity. The great barrier in their way is the Catholic Church. They are now openly conspiring for its overthrow.

In England our old craters are extinct and the mountains are quiet. Such a conflict has, happily, not yet been rekindled among us. No change on the part of the Catholic Church, of a kind to provoke such a conflict, either has been or will be made. The declining to accept a scheme of education based on principles dangerous to Catholic Faith is certainly no such cause. To reject a tempting gift is no aggression. If we are again to be distracted by religious conflicts, the responsibility will rest undividedly upon the head of anyone who shall break our present public confidence and peace. And that misdeed would be indelibly written in our history.

CHAPTER IV.

TRUE AND FALSE PROGRESS.

I WILL now go on to the fourth proposition—that by these collisions with the Church the Civil Powers everywhere are at this time destroying the first principle of their own stability.

Mr. Gladstone has represented me as saying that 'the civil order of all Christendom is the offspring of the Temporal Power, and has the Temporal Power for its keystone; that on the destruction of the Temporal Power "the laws of nations would at once fall in ruins."'

Understood as I wrote these words I fully affirm them; understood as they may be in this garbled form, they have an exaggeration which is not mine. I was speaking strictly of the Temporal Power of the Pope over his own State: whereby, as a King among Kings, he sustained the Christian character of Sovereignty. I was not speaking of Temporal power over the Temporal Government of Princes. And I was speaking in defence at a time when every journal in the country, with hardly an exception, was day after day assailing, and I must add misrepresenting, the origin and office of the Temporal Government of the Pope. My own words were as follows:—

'Now, the last point on which I will dwell is this: that as the Church of God has created—and that specially through the action of the Supreme Pontiffs in their civil mission to the world—this vast and fair fabric of Christian Europe, so it has perpetually sustained it. I ask, what has given it coherence? What is it that has kept alive the governing principle among men, but that pure faith or knowledge of God which has gone forth from the Holy See, and has filled the whole circumference of Christendom? What has bound men together in the respect due to mutual rights, but that pure morality which was delivered to the Church to guard, and of which the Holy See is the supreme interpreter? These two streams—which, as St. Cyprian says in his treatise on the unity of the Church, are like the rays that flow from the sun, or like the streams that rise and break from the fountain—illuminated and inundated the whole Christian world. Now, I ask, what has preserved this in security, but the infallibility of the Church of God vested chiefly and finally in the person of the Vicar of Jesus Christ? It will rather belong to the next lecture to note how, by contrast, this may be proved, and how those nations, which have separated themselves from the Unity of the Catholic Church, and therefore are in opposition to the temporal sovereignty of Rome, have lost these two great principles of their preservation. I ask, then, what has preserved Christian Europe, but the principle of obedience—the precept of submission, which has been taught throughout the whole of its circuit by the Church of God, especially through the mouths of its Pontiffs? By them subjects have been taught obedience and rulers have learned justice. What, I ask, has limited monarchy? What has made monarchy a free institution, and supreme power compatible with the personal liberty of the people, but the limitations which the Holy See, acting through its Pontiffs, has imposed upon the Princes of the world? Does anybody doubt these two propositions? To them I would say, the Pontiffs, with their temporal power, have been accused of despotism; at least, then, let us give them the credit of having taught the people to submit. They have been also accused of tyranny over Princes; at least let us give them the honor of having taught Kings that their power is limited. The dread chimera at which the English people especially stands in awe,—the deposing power of the Pope,—what was it but that supreme arbitration, whereby the highest power in the world, the Vicar of the Incarnate Son of God, anointed high-priest and supreme temporal ruler (i.e. as Sovereign in his own State), sat in his tribunal impartially to judge between nation and nation, between people and prince, between sovereign and subject? The deposing power grew up by the providential action of God in the world, teaching subjects obedience and princes clemency.

'Now, in this twofold power of the Popes, which has been, I may say, the centre of the diplomacy of Christian Europe, we see the sacerdotal and royal powers vested in one person, the two powers of king and priest, which are the two conservative principles of the Christian world. All Christian kings and all Christian priests stand related to the one person who bears in fulness that twofold character; and it is by adherence to that one person as the centre of the civil and spiritual system, which grew up under his hand, that Christian Europe is preserved. I should say further, that, vast and solid as Christendom may seem, like a vault of stone, the temporal power of the Pope is the keystone; strike it out, and the family of nations would at once fall in ruins.'[1]

In the very same chapter from which Mr. Gladstone has quoted, at page 46, the following statements occur at pages 32 and 33:—

(1) 'Our Divine Lord committed to His Church and to His Vicar—the head on earth of that Church—

---

[1] *Temporal Power of the Popes*, lecture ii. pp. 44-47. (Burns, 1862.)

His *Spiritual* sovereignty, reserving to Himself His *Temporal* or providential sovereignty. . . . Therefore the *Spiritual sovereignty* of the Church is a Divine institution, and has a power *directly* ordained of God. (2) There are other powers in the world which are indirectly ordained of God—viz. all temporal sovereignties. . . . (3) By an indirect but Divine providence our Divine Lord has liberated His Vicar upon earth, in the plenitude of His Spiritual sovereignty, from all civil subjection. . . . (4) By the same Providence —indirect, indeed, but nevertheless Divine—our Lord clothed His Vicar with the possession of a patrimony. . . . (5) Upon the basis of this temporal possession our Lord has raised a temporal power by His indirect operation, and therefore the temporal power of the Pope is a Divine ordinance, having a Divine sanction, at least equally with every other sovereignty in the world.'[1] It may not be amiss to add, lest it should be thought that this statement is merely a private opinion, that the text from which I quote was translated into Italian, in Rome, in 1862, was examined by the censorship, and printed at the Propaganda press.

This is still my unchanged belief, confirmed by the twelve years since these words were spoken, and by the shattered state of Christian Europe in 1875. Now I am not afraid of defending the condensed statement of Donoso Cortes: 'The history of Civilisation is the history of Christianity; the history of Christianity is the history of the Church; the history of the Church is the history of the Pontiffs.' St. Augustine's work *De*

---
[1] *Temporal Power of the Popes*, pp. 32, 33.

Civitate Dei is enough to prove that the civilisation of the old world had run itself out by incurable corruption, and that the civilisation of the modern world is the new creation of Christianity. Two other witnesses would also prove this: St. Paul in his first chapter to the Romans, and Dr. Döllinger in his work on 'The Jewish and the Gentile Nations.' I am indeed one of those who still believe that we owe Christian homes to Christian marriage, that we owe Christian men to Christian homes, that we owe Christian nations to Christian men, and that the transmission of national Christianity depends on Christian education. We owe, therefore, the civilisation of Europe to Christian nations, and we owe the whole, not to 'modern thought,' but to Christianity.

Moreover, I know of no agent by which Christianity was thus brought to bear upon mankind but the Christian Church; and, lastly, the heads of the Christian Church were the chief legislators, guides, judges, and protectors of this Christian civilisation. I cannot think that Mr. Gladstone would deny this, or that we have read history, all this while, in an inverted sense.

But there is another sense in which the Temporal Power of the Popes—that is, their local sovereignty—has in an especial manner created modern Europe. To them and to the Civil Government of the Patrimonies of the Church, when the Byzantine Empire had ceased to protect the West, may be ascribed the Christendom of which Charlemagne was the first Temporal Head. From that germ the Christian civilisation of Europe has been propagated by Christian marriage, Christian education, and Christian faith. Until 'Luther's mighty trumpet' was blown it was bound together by unity of faith, unity of worship, and unity of jurisdiction under one Head, and that Head united in himself the twofold character of Christian Pontiff and Christian King. Luther's blast has brought this down at last. First, by regalism in Protestant nations; and, secondly, by revolution in Catholic States. The principles of 1789 are Lutheranism applied to politics. We have already reached the time of civil marriage, of secular education, and of States in their public life without Christianity. But let us not think that we have reached our place of rest. Luther's blast, I fear, has yet more to do. Faith is dying out of the public life and action of all Governments. There is hardly a Catholic or a Christian Government left. The people they govern are divided in religion, and 'the religious difficulty' forces them to become simply secular in legislation and in action. So long as there was a Christian world, the Head of the Christian Church was recognised as the Vicar of a Divine Master, and had a Temporal Power among Christian Sovereigns, and a sovereignty of his own; but now that the nations have become secular, and no longer recognise his sacred office, his direction in temporal things is rejected by their rejection of faith. I am not arguing or lamenting, but explaining our actual state. And what is now the state and condition of the Christian world? Where are the Christian laws which formed it in the beginning? I was not far wrong in saying that the Temporal Power of the Head of the Christian Church was the keystone of a world which has crumbled from its Christian unity into a dismembered array of secular and conflicting nations, of armed camps and retarded maturity. And it is with this 'progress and modern civilisation that the Roman Pontiff is invited to conform and to reconcile himself.' This is the sum and exposition of 'modern thought,' save only that it omits the Agnostic theology *De Deo non existente*, and the anthropology of Apes. Mr. Gladstone quotes this contemned proposition, recited in the Syllabus, as a *gravamen* against the Pope and the Catholics of these kingdoms. We have no desire to see the Christian Commonwealth of England decompose before our eyes under Luther's blast. We are content with the English Monarchy, founded and consolidated by our Catholic forefathers; and with our English Constitution, of which the solid and unshaken base and the dominant constructive lines are Christian and Catholic. We Englishmen were once perfectly one in faith. Luther's blast has given us nearly three hundred years of penal laws, bitter contentions, a 'bloody reign of Mary,' a relentless shower, indeed, between two seas of blood, in the reigns of her father and her sister; and when these horrors relaxed, streams of blood still flowed on for another hundred years. For nearly three centuries we have been divided in politics, because politics were mixed up with religion. Our Legislature teemed with penal laws such as the world had never seen, and that against nearly a half of the English population. We were weakened because we were divided; haunted by suspicions of conspiracy and scared by fancied dangers, because we were consciously doing wrong, as Prussia is at this day. But now for fifty years we have had peace, because we have common interests, and a solid common weal. The three Kingdoms are without anxiety and without fear. And why? Because we have eliminated religious conflicts from our Legislation, because we have learned to be just, because we have learned also that the Civil Ruler may punish what men do, but not what men think, unless they issue in acts against the State. All men, so far as conscience and faith extend, are now equal before the law. No man is molested for his religion. Although this is not the golden age of unity in truth, which the Christian Church once created and Pius IX. declares to be the only civilisation and the only progress to which he can conform himself, though he tolerates what he cannot cure; nevertheless, it is a silver age in which we can peacefully accept what we cannot either justify as the will of God, or extol as the normal state of the Christian world. In our shattered state of religious belief and worship there is no way of solid civil peace, but in leaving all men free in their amplest liberty of faith. It is because this is vital to our welfare as an Empire, and because, as it seems to me, the late sudden and needless aggression on the Catholic religion is dangerous to the social and political tranquillity of these Kingdoms, that I have pointed to Germany, as a warning. A monarchy of a thousand years is a majestic thing in this modern world of fleeting dynasties and of chronic revolutions. We possess a royal lineage the least broken and the most closely united to the people that the world has ever seen, save one. The line of Pontiffs ruled before the crowned heads of to-day came into existence. It has been the vital chord of the Christian people of the world.

Next after the line of Pontiffs, there is nothing in history more time-honored or grander than the Monarchy of Alfred, which reigns to this day. Does Mr. Gladstone think that the Vatican Council binds me to desire its overthrow? Next to seeing again the laws and the faith of good King Edward restored throughout the land, we desire to see the Sovereign of England reigning by equal laws over a people united at least in everything that is right and just and lawful in this world, if indeed they must still be in higher laws and truths divided.

One thing is most certain, Catholics will never lend so much as a finger or a vote to overturn by political action the Christianity which still lingers in our public laws. They will cherish all of it that remains in our popular education. If we could see the tradition of our national Christianity healed of its wounds and taken up into the full life and unity of perfect faith by the spiritual forces of conviction and of persuasion, as that supernatural unity was created in the beginning, we should rejoice with thanksgiving; but no Catholic will diminish by a shade the Christianity which still survives. We cannot, indeed, co-operate by any direct action to uphold what we believe to be erroneous; but it will find no political hostility in us. They who wish its overthrow would pull it down not for what we think erroneous in it, but for what is true; and what is true in it we revere as the truth of God. In our divided religious state the public revenues, once paid into the treasury, have passed beyond the individual conscience. Thenceforward they fall under the impartial administration of our mixed commonwealth. I am not responsible for the application of them. My conscience is not touched if public revenues are given to a Presbyterian or to a Baptist School. My conscience is not ill at ease even if grants are made to a school in which no religion at all is taught. A people divided in religion pays its taxes, and a Parliament divided in religion votes the public money by an equitable balance for our manifold uses in the midst of our manifold divisions. No one has a right to control this mixed administration to satisfy his private conscience, or to claim to have it all his own way. No Secularist can regard my schools with more aversion than I regard his; but I am passive when he receives his share of the public money. I trust the day will never come when any one section or sect among us shall gain a domination over the equities which render tolerable our divided state. I hope no Puritans will rise up again to do in England, by the help of Secularists and unbelievers, what they did in Maryland. There they destroyed the fairest promise of peace that a wrecked world ever saw. England at this time is Maryland upon an imperial scale. He who shall break our religious peace will go down to history with those whose names Englishmen try to forget.

It is for this reason that I lament when six millions of British subjects are told by a voice of great authority that they are loyal indeed, but in spite of their religion. When men are so taught they are very apt to learn the lesson. They will be ready to say, if by my whole life I am loyal, but by my religion I ought, as I am told, to be disloyal, I am, therefore, either a traitor or a heretic. If I am a heretic I shall lose my soul; but for imputed treason I can only lose my life. If men of Mr. Gladstone's age and fame say these things, the masses will be very apt to believe them. And if he should also say that Pius IX. and the whole Episcopate, and the Vatican Council, and the Clergy of England and Ireland, so believe and teach, I can hardly find fault with a plain man who says, 'Your arguments and quotations are above me, but I know that the Pope and the Church cannot mislead me; they must know the Catholic faith better than you. At all costs I must believe them.' I could not blame such a man in refusing for so obvious a reason to listen to Mr. Gladstone when he expostulates with the Vatican Council. Indeed, I can conceive that it will not promote loyalty in England or Ireland to hold up passages from books written even by me in proof that Catholics must choose between their loyalty and their religion. They may be more likely to choose to err even with me than to correct their faith at the voice of any politician. Moreover, they may even be tempted to think that if I am not loyal they need not be. It is a dangerous thing to tell a flock of many millions that the Pastors they trust are, or ought to be, disloyal. They will be apt to say, 'We do not understand it; but if it be true, there must be some very strong and sufficient reason.' I can conceive that the Catholic peasants in Germany may have argued in this plain way, even before they understood the merits of the cause. They saw the Archbishop of Posen carried off to prison. Depend upon it their confidence went with him. This is playing with edged tools, and in a matter where it is hardly moral to play at all. Great public disasters might be caused by the game, and the costs of the game would fall, not upon the gamester, but upon innocent men, and women, and children.

I could not refrain from saying thus much of England. But I have little fear that the stream of our equal legislation will be turned aside, much less turned back; or that our public peace will be broken. The destinies of the British Empire are in strong hands, guided by calm heads, and supported by a balanced and steady public opinion, which in the last two months has manifested a self-command and an equity which do honour to our country.

As to Germany I shall say no more. Luther's might trumpet has already rung twice through Germany. It rang long and loud from 1535 to 1542, and again longer and louder from 1618 to 1648. The old Germany that heard it has ceased to exist.[1] God grant that it may not give such notes again. Everyone who bears a human heart, and a love for the Christian world and a good-will to Germany, will share in this desire.

But if the conflicts of Governments against the Church are fatal to the public peace and to themselves, as assuredly they would be to the British Empire if our accusers should rekindle old strifes, and as they assuredly will be in the German Empire, whether the policy of Prince Von Bismarck fail or succeed, there can be found no sadder example of this disastrous imprudence in statesmen than in the case of Italy. For eight and twenty years a wanton and mischievous ag-

---

[1] See Archbishop Trench's *Gustavus Adolphus*, pp. 88, 89, 161.

gression against the Holy See has been carried on. I say wanton, because it has been without a cause. I say mischievous, because it has retarded and endangered the unity and independence of Italy, and the public and private prosperity of the Italian people. As Mr. Gladstone has reviewed his relation to the Italian question in its bearing on his Expostulation, I may do the same.

At the outset of their task of unifying and vindicating the independence of Italy, the Italian politicians began by assailing the principle of all unity among men. They engaged all the pride and all the passion of Italy in a deadly conflict with the special source of all its greatness. Had they worked from that centre of their moral life, Italy at this day would have been united, peaceful, and strong. These are, indeed, my convictions, but not my words. Neither the present party which rules Italy, nor the party which has encouraged them in this country, will, perhaps, listen to me. But they will listen, I hope, to one who was an Italian, and a lover of the unity and independence of Italy. Vincenzo Gioberti, in his 'Primato degli Italiani,' after proving that religion is the source of all civilisation, says:—

'If, then, the whole culture of a people has its impulse and origin from religion, how can we treat of its culture without speaking of its religion? If the culture of Europe in general, and that of Italy in particular, were the work of the New Rome and of its belief, how is it possible to discuss this twofold argument, and to be silent about Catholicism and about the Pope? In writing a book upon Italy I protest that I desire to speak of the living and real Italy as it exists at this day, not of the Italy that is dead these fourteen hundred years, nor of an abstract allegorical Italy that is not to be found in the outward world, but only in the brain of some philosopher.' . . . 'Italy is differenced from the Gentile nations by its Christianity; from those that are in heresy and schism by its Catholicism; and from the other nations which are Catholic by the fact that it is placed in the centre of Catholicism, and not in the outline or circumference.' . . . 'But among the Catholic populations, the Italian has the privilege of occupying the first place, because it possesses in its heart the first See.

'I hope that these suggestions will be enough to justify the small amount of theology that I have put into this book.'. . . Two facts seem to me conspicuous in the political (*civile*) world at this day ' . . . 'the first is the exclusion of the Theology of Revelation from the field of the Encyclopedia of human knowledge; the second is the removal of the Catholic clergy from the influence in civil affairs.' . . . . 'I count it to be the duty of a writer, above all if he be a philosopher, Catholic and Italian, to combat these two grand aberrations of modern civilisation, and to recall things to their first principles; endeavouring to restore the universal primacy of religion in the circle of things and of knowledge.' . . . . 'I therefore do not believe that I deceive myself in affirming that every scientific reform is vain, if it do not make chief account of religion, and that every scheme of Italian renovation is null, if it have not for its base the corner-stone of Catholicism.'[1]

After a contrast of the theoretical abstractions of the Ghibelline party and the practical and popular policy of the Guelphs, Gioberti continues :—

'The Italy of that day was not the Italy of the ancient Latins, corrupted by the incapacity of the later Emperors, and

[1] Gioberti, *Primato degli Italiani*, vol. ii. pp. 28–31.

destroyed by the ferocity of the northern barbarians. In its stead a new Rome had been created, under the auspices, not of Romulus, but of Peter, not of the Conscript Fathers of old Rome, but of the Episcopate, and of the councils which are the Patrician order and the Senate of the universal Christendom. The Guelphs, therefore, did not separate the civil constitution of Italy from the Pontificate, and, without confounding the human order with the divine, they believed that God, having privileged the Peninsula with the first See of the faith, mother of all others . . . . it ought to exercise the chief part in the political order of Italy.' . . . 'But in this day many think otherwise, and in their opinion the Pope has about as much to do with the national condition of Italy as he has with that of China. This comes from the weakness into which foreign influences have led the Papacy, and from the springing up again for the last century of the ancient spirit of the Nominalists and the Ghibellines, under the form of Gallicanism, Jansenism, Cartesianism, Voltairianism, or under the disguise of rationalism and German pantheism, prompted by the same principles, and springing from the same countries respectively as those former heresies. And the evil will last as long as men persist in substituting a heathen or chimerical Italy in the place of a real and a Christian Italy, which God, and a life of eighteen hundred years, has created; that is to say, a French or German Italy in the place of an Italy of the Italians. But I cannot understand how men can ascribe the civilisation of Europe in general to Christianity (of which there is at this day no writer of any force who doubts), and not award in particular the culture of our Peninsula to the Holy See; for the Pope is to the universal Church that which the civilisation of Italy is to that of Europe.'[1]

[1] Gioberti, *Primato degli Italiani*, vol. ii. pp. 66, 67.

I will add but one more passage, which will enunciate in the words of an Italian patriot the affirmation I have made :—

'The separating of the national personality of Italy from its religious principle, and from the dignity which spreads throughout it from the Christian monarchy of which it is the home (*residenza*), is not, in my opinion, the least of the causes which, for many centuries, weakens the minds of Italians. This error sprung in part from the habit of arguing and judging of Christian Italy after the manner of pagans, and in part from the custom of reasoning, according to the canons of a philosophy which is governed, not by rational ideas nor by living and concrete facts, but by empty abstractions.'[1]

Such was the estimate of a man who loved Italy with all his heart, and desired to see it united, and independent of all foreign dynasties.

This is no mere speculation as to what the Catholic religion and the Pope may be to Italy, but a strict historical fact. The Pontiffs have been for fourteen hundred years the chief popular power in Italy. I say popular, not dynastic; not despotic, but Guelf. In the fifth century the Pontiffs saved Italy from the Gothic invasions. St. Innocent I. saved Ravenna and Rome. St. Leo saved Italy from Attila, and Rome from Genseric. In the sixth and seventh centuries St. Gregory was the chief defender of Italy and Rome against the Lombards. The same is true in the time of Gregory II. and Adrian I. In the ninth, tenth, and eleventh centuries the Pontiffs Leo IV. and Gregory IV. saved Italy from the Saracens. So also John VIII., John X.,

[1] Gioberti, *Primato degli Italiani*, vol. ii. pp. 60.

Benedict VIII. beat back the Saracens, and finally drove them from Sardinia. The Crusades of Urban II. and St. Pius V. saved Italy and Europe from the Mohammedan Power. In the great contest about Investitures, the Pontiffs, from Gregory VII. to Calistus II., saved the Church from subjection to the Empire, and Italy from subjection to Germany. The ecclesiastical and political liberties of Italy were both at stake, and were both vindicated together by the action of the Pontiffs. In the twelfth and thirteenth centuries the liberty of the Italian Communes was saved from the feudal despotism of the Hohenstaufen by the Popes. Alexander III. and the Lombard League defended popular liberty against Frederick Barbarossa. The City of Alexandria is to this day the monument of the gratitude of the Lombard people. The City of Cæsarea has ceased to exist. Innocent III. and the Tuscan League saved the liberties of Central Italy. Gregory IX. and Innocent IV. resisted the tyranny of Frederick II., and finally saved the independence of Italy from the Imperial despotism. Then came the contest of the people and the Empire, the Guelfs and the Ghibellines. In these conflicts the Popes and the people were indivisible. In the fourteenth and fifteenth centuries the Popes were the soul and the strength of the Italian Leagues, whereby the people and their liberties were protected from the enormities of tyrants and adventurers and Free Companies. In the fifteenth century Nicholas V. maintained peace among the Princes and people of Italy, and drew Naples, Milan, Florence, Venice, and Genoa into a Confederation to maintain the Italian independence.

Pius II. protected, in like manner, the liberty of Italy from the intrusions of France. Paul II. leagued together all the Princes of Italy in defence of Italian freedom. Julius II. laboured to drive all foreign domination out of Italy. Leo X. made it his chief policy to liberate Italy from all foreign dominion, and to unite all the Princes of Italy in a Confederation of independence.

Paul IV., though unsuccessful, was the champion of the independence of Italy against the Spaniards. From that time onwards the Pontiffs were ever in conflict against Spain or France to save the liberties of Italy and of the Church. The histories of Pius VI. and Pius VII. are too well known to need recital.

It is therefore too late in the day to go about to persuade men that the Pontiffs were ever opposed to Italian unity, Italian freedom, Italian independence. These three things have been the aim and the work of the whole line of Popes, down to Pius IX. Even Mr. Gladstone acknowledges that Pius IX. is 'an Italian.'[1] Beyond all doubt there is not one in the long line I have quoted who has loved Italy more than he. There is not one who had at heart more ardently the unity, freedom, and independence of Italy. His first act was to set free every political prisoner with a full pardon. By that act he showed that he recognised the misdirected love of country in those who had been seduced into false or unlawful ways of seeking the unity and the liberties of their country.

In 1847 Pius IX. invited all the Princes of Italy to

[1] *Expostulation*, p. 49.

a League of Customs, by which the principle of Federal Unity would have been established. From this germ the National Unity would have steadily grown up, without shock or overthrow of right or justice. Once confederated, there was no identity of interests, no unity of power, which might not have grown solid and mature. This and the Supreme Council for the Government of the Pontifical State are proof enough of his desire for Italian unity, and of the far-reaching foresight with which he aimed at the elevation of Italy. And as for Italian independence, let the following letter, written by himself to the Emperor of Austria on the 2nd of May, 1848, suffice:—

'Your Imperial Majesty, this Holy See has been always wont to speak words of peace in the midst of the wars that stain the Christian world with blood; and in our Allocution of the 29th of last month, while we declared that our paternal heart shrunk from declaring war, we expressly declared our ardent desire to restore peace. Let it not be displeasing, therefore, to your Majesty that we turn to your piety and religion, and exhort you with a father's affection to withdraw your armies from a war which, while it cannot reconquer to the Empire the hearts of the Lombards and Venetians, draws after it the lamentable series of calamities that ever accompany warfare, and are assuredly abhorred and detested by you. Let it not be displeasing to the generous German people, that we invite them to lay aside all hatreds and to turn a domination which could not be either noble or happy while it rests only on the sword, into the useful relations of friendly neighborhood. Thus we trust that the German nation, honorably proud of its own nationality, will not engage its honor in sanguinary attempts against the Italian nation, but will place it rather in nobly acknowledging it as a sister, as indeed both nations are our daughters, and most dear to our heart; thereby mutually withdrawing to dwell each one in its natural boundaries with honorable treaties and the benediction of the Lord. Meanwhile, we pray to the Giver of all lights and the Author of all good to inspire your Majesty with holy counsels, and give from our inmost heart to you and Her Majesty the Empress, and to the Imperial family, the Apostolic benediction.

'Given in Rome at Santa Maria Maggiore, on the third day of May, in the year 1848, the second of our Pontificate.

PIUS PP. IX.'

The following passage, from an impartial observer, will attest what were the intentions and desires of Pius IX. :—

'The opposition of Austria has been constant and intense from the moment of his election. The spectacle of an Italian Prince, relying for the maintenance of his power on the affectionate regard and the national sympathies of his people; the resolution of the Pope to pursue a course of moderate reform, to encourage railroads, to emancipate the press, to admit laymen to offices in the State, and to purify the law; but, above all, the dignified independence of action manifested by the Court of Rome, have filled the Austrians with exasperation and apprehension. There is not the least doubt that the Cabinet of Vienna is eager to grasp at the slightest pretext for an armed intervention south of the Po. If such a pretext do not occur, it is but too probable that it may be created; and any disturbances calculated to lead to such a result would at once betray their insidious origin. Meanwhile, the Pope is menaced in Austrian notes, which have sometimes transgressed the limits of policy and decorum; and the minor Princes of Italy are terrified by extravagant intimations of hostile designs entertained against them by the National Party, headed by the Pope and the House of Savoy, in order to persuade them that their only safeguard is the Austrian army. These intrigues may be thought necessary to the defence of the tottering power of Austria south of the Alps, for every step made in advance by Italy is a step towards the emancipation of the country.'[1]

But the evil genius of revolution had begun to work. Across the field of the Christian and Catholic traditions of Italy, a chimerical theory of a Communistic State, a Republic without Christianity, a democracy without King or Pontiff, forced itself.

Mazzini had been crying for years, 'The Papacy is extinct, Catholicism is a corpse, and the Pope knows this. .... Read the Evangelical Letter.'[2] He had taught Young Italy the three degrees, of Guerilla Bands, Insurrection, Revolution.[3] The mine was charged and the fuse already lighted. This widespread Secret Association covered the face of Italy. What followed all men know: the murder of Rossi, the siege of the Quirinal Palace, the wreck of all authority, the Socialist Revolution, the Roman Republic, impunity of sacrilege, and a reign of terror.

Now, let us suppose that in the period of our history, when the unity of the English people was gradually consolidating, some organised Apostleship of Socialism had begun to whisper in private and to preach in public such doctrines of conspiracy as these, and to teach that the people could never be free so long as King or Priest existed; that all monarchical power

[1] *Times*, March 28, 1847.
[2] *Life and Writings of Mazzini*, vol. i. p. 248.
[3] *Ibid.* p. 108, and Appendix, 1864.

and ecclesiastical authority were enemies of the public weal; that the overthrow of the Monarchy and the extinction of the Church were the only remedies of present evils, the only means of future progress. Such a foreign element of discord, mistrust, conspiracy would have divided the hearts, intellects, and wills of the people of England, and rendered its unification impossible. The unity of religion in faith and worship, the unity of the Spiritual authority which spoke to the reason and the will of men, was then, as it is at this hour, the only principle of unity. Without this, legislation is merely mechanical; a dynamic power is wanted to bind men into one people. Our forefathers had it, and the English Monarchy of a thousand years is its fruit. The Italians have it at this hour in great vividness; but Philosophers and Doctrinaires, Conspirators and Communists, are perverting the intellect and dividing the wills of the rising men of Italy. If such a conspiracy had crossed our early unification, we should have been, it may be, at this day, I will not say a Heptarchy, but assuredly a divided people, with a paralyzed national will. May God save Italy from this danger. It is not too late. It was said in an eloquent speech, the other day, that a people which breaks with its past is doomed to division and to instability. The rupture of France with its ancient traditions in 1789 has generated the brood of political parties, which, from month to month, thwart and defeat each other's action, like palsied limbs. If Italy should break with its past; if it should forget the labours, and sufferings, and dangers which united its Pontiffs and its people in the wars of its independence, freedom, and unity; if it should forget the confederations wrought by the Pontiffs, by which they made all the divisions of Italy work together for the liberties of the whole Peninsula, from the Alps to its foot—then, indeed, I should despair of its future. It could have no other in store than a chronic warfare of parties, and the final sway of some successful soldier.

Of the population of 26,000,000 Italians not three millions have launched themselves in the revolution of the last twenty years. The great bulk of the people are, as they have always been, Christian, Catholic, and loyal. The Electoral body who have votes to return the Italian Parliament do not exceed in number some half million. Of these hardly one-half record their vote. The Italian Deputies are, therefore, chosen by one-hundredth part of the population. The whole Chamber is, therefore, revolutionary, and may be divided into two parties—the moderate revolution and the extreme revolution. The Catholic voters abstain from all participation in such a state. They are not revolutionists, either extreme or moderate. They could elect no deputy but one of their own principles; and no such deputy could sit, because to take his place he must bind himself by oath to the existing state of things, including, therefore, the violation of the sovereignty of the Pontiff. More than this, the existing state of the law has invaded the liberties and jurisdiction of the Church. It has abolished religious orders and institutions, it has harshly turned out their inmates upon a pittance, which, if paid, would not suffice for food. It has confiscated property, seized upon colleges, abolished theology from

the universities, and the Christian doctrine from
schools. And all this, be it remembered, not to meet
the distracted state of a people who have lost their religious unity, and must be provided with civil marriage
and secular education, but in the midst of a population
absolutely and universally Catholic. This, and not
what Mr. Gladstone, with a strange want of accuracy,
supposes, is what the Syllabus condemns. It nowhere
condemns the civil policy which is necessary for a people hopelessly divided in religion. For us this may be
a necessity. In Italy it is a doctrine of the Doctrinaires. To force upon the united people of Italy that
which is necessary for the divided people of England is
a senseless legislation, and a mischievous breaking with
the glorious past of Italy. I do not now stay to dwell
upon the unpatriotic and un-Italian agitation of men
who for twenty-five years have threatened Pius IX.
with violence, and assailed him as the Vampire, the
Canker, the Gangrene of Italy. Such men, from Aspro-
monte to this day, have been the chief hindrance to the
unification and pacification of Italy. And those who in
this country have encouraged and abetted those agita-
tors—not that they knew anything but that Garibaldi
was fighting against the Pope—have been among the
worst friends of Italy ; I might say among the uncon-
scious but most mischievous enemies. It is strange
how this one taint of bigotry will pervert everything.
Garibaldi was raising insurrection in Sicily and Naples
against a lawful sovereign ; and those who put us now
to question about our loyalty cheered and aided him by
all moral influence. More than this, when the leader of
rebellion came to England he was received with royal

honours, and red carpets were spread for him at the threshold of aristocratic houses, until his name was found to be contagious. Then, in twenty-four hours he was sped from England with the profuse facilities of departure which wait upon an unwelcome guest. In my judgment—and I have formed it not in London from newspaper correspondents, but in Rome during many a long residence, extending in all over seven years—those who have encouraged this chronic agitation against the religion of Italians and the independence of Rome, have been among the chief causes of the present disorders of Italy. They could put no surer bar to its unity or to the solution of the Roman question which they confidently believe to be settled. They are keeping it open by encouraging the Government of the day to persist in quarrelling with the Catholic Church and with its Head. But this part of the subject has outgrown its proportion. I return, therefore, to the proposition I set out to prove,—that by the collisions which now exist between the Civil Powers and the Church, the Governments of Europe are destroying the main principle of their own stability. And I must add that they who are rekindling the old fires of religious discord in such an equal and tempered Commonwealth as ours, seem to me to be serving neither God nor their country.

CHAPTER V.

THE MOTIVE OF THE DEFINITION.

My last proposition is that the motive of the Council of the Vatican for defining the Infallibility of the Roman Pontiff was not any temporal motive, nor was it for temporal ends; but that the Definition was made in the face of all temporal dangers, in order to guard the Divine deposit of Christianity, and to vindicate the Divine certainty of Faith.

I have read many things in Mr. Gladstone's pamphlet which are unlike himself, but none seems more so to me than this question, 'Why did that Court, with policy for ever in its eye, lodge such formidable demands for power of the vulgar kind in that sphere which is visible, and where hard knocks can undoubtedly be given as well as received?'[1]

Would it not have been more seemly and more dignified if the question had been couched in some such words as these: 'Why has the Catholic Church, in a moment of great peril, when a revolution is at the gates of Rome, and the Civil Powers of the world are uniting, not only to forsake it, but even to threaten it with opposition—why has it at such a time, in spite of every inducement of policy, and every motive of interest, and in defiance of every pleading of worldly wisdom, persisted in defining the Infallibility

[1] *Expostulation*, p. 47.

of the Pope—a doctrine which is sure to bring down upon the Church the animosities of all its enemies without, and the conspiracies of all its faithless members within?' Even Mr. Gladstone can see that this was most impolitic. Why, then, will he accuse the Church of always having a policy in its eye? By his own confession it is not always so: for he is witness that it is not so in this case. Why, then, would he not say so? I will gladly answer the question he has put.

The reasons, then, why the Infallibility of the Roman Pontiff ought to be defined were publicly stated as follows, in 1869, before the Vatican Council met; and some or all of them, I believe, prevailed in determining the Council to make that definition:—

'Those who maintain that the time is ripe, and that such a definition would be opportune, justify their opinion on the following reasons:—

'1. Because the doctrine of the Infallibility of the Vicar of Jesus Christ, speaking *ex cathedra*, in matter of faith and morals, is true.

'2. Because this truth has been denied.

'3. Because this denial has generated extensive doubt as to the truth of this doctrine, which lies at the root of the immemorial and universal practice of the Church, and therefore at the foundation of Christianity in the world.

'4. Because this denial, if it arose informally about the time of the Council of Constance, has been revived, and has grown into a formal and public error since the closing of the last General Council.

'5. Because, if the next General Council shall pass it over, the error will henceforward appear to be tolerated, or at least left in impunity; and the Pontifical censures of Innocent XI., Alexander VIII., Innocent XII., and Pius VI. will appear to be of doubtful effect.

'6. Because this denial of the traditional belief of the Church is not a private, literary, and scholastic opinion; but a patent, active, and organised opposition to the prerogatives of the Holy See.

'7. Because this erroneous opinion has gravely enfeebled the doctrinal authority of the Church in the minds of a certain number of the faithful; and if passed over in impunity, this ill effect will be still further encouraged.

'8. Because this erroneous opinion has at times caused and kept open a theological and practical division among pastors and people; and has given occasion to domestic criticisms, mistrusts, animosities, and alienations.

'9. Because these divisions tend to paralyse the action of truth upon the minds of the faithful *ad intra;* and, consequently, by giving a false appearance of division and doubt among Catholics, upon the minds of Protestants and others *ad extra.*

'10. Because, as the absence of a definition gives occasion for these separations and oppositions of opinion among pastors and people, so, if defined, the doctrine would become a basis and a bond of unity among the faithful.

'11. Because, if defined in an Œcumenical Council, the doctrine would be at once received throughout the world, both by those who believe the Infallibility of the Pontiff and by those who believe the Infallibility of the Church, and with the same universal joy and unanimity as the definition of the Immaculate Conception.

'12. Because the definition of the ordinary means whereby the faith is proposed to the world is required to complete the treatise "De Fide Divina."

'13. Because the same definition is required to complete the treatise "De Ecclesia, deque Dotibus ejus."

'14. Because it is needed to place the Pontifical Acts during the last three hundred years, both in declaring the truth, as in the dogma of the Immaculate Conception, and in condemning errors, as in the long series of propositions condemned in Baius, Jansenius, and others, beyond cavil or question; and still more, to make manifest that the active Infallibility of the Church, between council and council, is not dormant, suspended, or intermittent; and to exclude the heretical supposition that infallible decrees are left to the exposition and interpretation of a fallible judge.

'15. Because the full and final declaration of the divine authority of the Head of the Church is needed to exclude from the minds of pastors and faithful the political influences which have generated Gallicanism, Imperialism, Regalism, and Nationalism, the perennial sources of error, contention, and schism.

'For these, and for many more reasons which it is impossible now to detail, many believe that a definition or declaration which would terminate this long and pernicious question, would be opportune; and that it might for ever be set at rest by the condemnation of the propositions following:—

'1. That the decrees of the Roman Pontiffs in matter of faith and morals do not oblige the conscience unless they be made in a General Council, or before they obtain at least the tacit consent of the Church.

'2. That the Roman Pontiff, when he speaks in matter of faith and morals, as the universal Doctor and Teacher of the Church, may err.'[1]

I will now, as briefly as I can, state what the Definition is. The greater part of the excitement and alarm on this subject arises from a want of just and clear perception of what the doctrine of Infallibility signifies. .

'The fourth and last chapter of the "Constitution on the Church" defines the infallible doctrinal authority of the Roman Pontiff as the supreme teacher of all Christians.

'The chapter opens by affirming that to this supreme jurisdiction is attached a proportionate grace, whereby its exercise is directed and sustained.

'This truth has been traditionally held and taught by the Holy See, by the *praxis* of the Church, and by the Œcumenical Councils, especially those in which the East and the West met in union together; as, for instance, the fourth of Constantinople, the second of Lyons, and the Council of Florence.

'It is then declared that, in virtue of the promise of our Lord, "I have prayed for thee, that thy faith fail not,"[2] a perpetual grace of stability in faith was Divinely attached to Peter and to his successors in his See.

---

[1] *Petri Privilegium*, part ii. pp. 119–122. (Longmans, 1869.)
[2] St. Luke xxii. 31, 32.

'The definition then affirms "that the Roman Pontiff, when he speaks *ex cathedra*—that is, when in discharge of the office of Pastor and Doctor of all Christians, by virtue of his supreme Apostolic authority, he defines a doctrine regarding faith or morals to be held by the Universal Church—by the Divine assistance promised to him in Blessed Peter, is possessed of that Infallibility with which the Divine Redeemer willed that His Church should be endowed for defining doctrine regarding faith and morals; and that, therefore, such definitions of the Roman Pontiff are irreformable of themselves, and not from the consent of the Church.

'In this definition there are six points to be noted:

'First, it defines the meaning of the well-known phrase, *loquens ex cathedra;* that is, speaking from the seat, or place, or with the authority of, the supreme teacher of all Christians, and binding the assent of the Universal Church.

'Secondly, the subject-matter of his infallible teaching; namely, the doctrine of faith and morals.

'Thirdly, the efficient cause of Infallibility; that is, the Divine assistance promised to Peter, and in Peter to his successors.

'Fourthly, the act to which this Divine assistance is attached; namely, the *defining* of doctrines of faith and morals.

'Fifthly, the extension of this infallible authority to the limits of the doctrinal office of the Church.

'Lastly, the dogmatic value of the definitions *ex cathedra;* namely, that they are in themselves irreformable, because in themselves infallible, and not because the Church, or any part or member of the Church, should assent to them.

'These six points contain the whole definition of Infallibility.

'I. First, the definition limits the Infallibility of the Pontiff to the acts which emanate from him *ex cathedra*. This phrase, which has been long and commonly used by theologians, has now, for the first time, been adopted into the terminology of the Church, and in adopting it the Vatican Council fixes its meaning. The Pontiff speaks *ex cathedra* when, and only when, he speaks as the Pastor and Doctor of all Christians. By this all acts of the Pontiff as a private person, or a private doctor, or as a local bishop, or as sovereign of a State, are excluded.[1] In all these acts the Pontiff may be subject to error. In one and one only capacity he is exempt from error; that is, when, as teacher of the whole Church, he teaches the whole Church in things of faith and morals.

'Our Lord declared "Super Cathedram Moysi sederunt Scribæ et Pharisæi—the Scribes and Pharisees have sat in the chair of Moses." The seat or *cathedra* of Moses signifies the authority and the doctrine of Moses; the *cathedra Petri* is in like manner the autho-

[1] Cardinal Sfondrati, writing in 1684, explained this truth as follows:—'The Pontiff does some things as man, some as prince, some as doctor, some as pope; that is, as head and foundation of the Church; and it is only to these (last-named) actions that we attribute the gift of Infallibility. The others we leave to his human condition. As, then, not every action of the Pope is papal, so not every action of the Pope enjoys the papal privilege. This, therefore, is to act as Pontiff, and to speak *ex cathedra*, which is not within the competency of any (other) doctor or bishop.'—*Regale Sacerdotium*, lib. iii. sec. 1.

rity and doctrine of Peter. The former was binding by Divine command, and under pain of sin, upon the people of God under the Old Law; the latter is binding by Divine command, and under pain of sin, upon the people of God under the New.

'I need not here draw out the traditional use of the term *cathedra Petri*, which in St. Cyprian, St. Optatus, and St. Augustine, is employed as synonymous with the successor of Peter, and is used to express the centre and test of Catholic unity. *Ex cathedra* is therefore equivalent to *ex cathedra Petri*, and distinguishes those acts of the successors of Peter which are done as supreme teacher of the whole Church.

'The value of this phrase is great, inasmuch as it excludes all cavil and equivocation as to the acts of the Pontiff in any other capacity than that of supreme Doctor of all Christians, and in any other subject-matter than the matters of faith and morals.

'II. Secondly, the definition limits the range, or, to speak exactly, the object of Infallibility, to the doctrine of faith and morals. It excludes, therefore, all other matter whatsoever.

'The great commission or charter of the Church is, in the words of our Lord, "Go ye therefore and teach all nations . . . . teaching them to observe all things whatsoever I have commanded you; and behold I am with you all days, even to the consummation of the world."[1]

'In these words are contained five points:

'First, the perpetuity and universality of the mission of the Church as the teacher of mankind.

[1] St. Matt. xxviii. 19, 20

'Secondly, the deposit of the Truth and of the Commandments, that is, of the Divine Faith and Law entrusted to the Church.

'Thirdly, the office of the Church, as the sole interpreter of the Faith and of the Law.

'Fourthly, that it has the sole Divine jurisdiction existing upon earth, in matters of salvation, over the reason and the will of man.

'Fifthly, that, in the discharge of this office, our Lord is with His Church always, and to the consummation of the world.

'The doctrine of faith and the doctrine of morals are here explicitly described. The Church is infallible in this deposit of revelation.

'And in this deposit are truths and morals both of the natural and of the supernatural order; for the religious truths and morals of the natural order are taken up into the revelation of the order of grace, and form a part of the object of Infallibility.

'The phrase, then, "faith and morals" signifies the whole revelation of faith; the whole way of salvation through faith; or the whole supernatural order, with all that is essential to the sanctification and salvation of man through Jesus Christ.

'This formula is variously expressed by the Church and by theologians; but it always means one and the same thing.

'The Fourteenth Œcumenical Council of Lyons in 1274 says, "If any questions arise concerning faith, they are to be decided by the Roman Pontiff."[1]

---

[1] 'Si quæ subortæ fuerint quæstiones de fide, suo (i.e. Rom. Pont.) debent judicio definiri.'—Labbe, *Concil.* tom. xiv. p. 512, Venice, 1731.

'The Council of Trent uses the formula "In things of faith and morals pertaining to the edification of Christian doctrine."[1] . . . .

'The object of Infallibility, therefore, is the whole revealed Word of God; and all that is so in contact with revealed truth, that without treating of it the Word of God could not be guarded, expounded, and defended. As, for instance, in declaring the Canon, and authenticity, and true interpretation of Holy Scripture, and the like.

'Further, it is clear that the Church has an infallible guidance, not only in all matters that are revealed, but also in all matters which are opposed to revelation. For the Church could not discharge its office as the Teacher of all nations, unless it were able with infallible certainty to proscribe doctrines at variance with the Word of God.

'From this, again, it follows that the *direct* object of Infallibility is the Revelation, or Word, of God; the *indirect* object is whatsoever is necessary for its exposition or defence, and whatsoever is contrariant to the Word of God, that is, to faith and morals. The Church, having a Divine office to condemn errors in faith and morals, has therefore an infallible assistance in discerning and proscribing false philosophies and false science.[2] . . .

[1] 'In rebus fidei et morum ad ædificationem doctrinæ Christianæ pertinentium.'—Sess. iv. *Decret. de Edit. et Usu Sac. Lib.*

[2] 'Further, the Church, which, together with the Apostolic office of teaching, has received a charge to guard the deposit of faith, derives from God the right and the duty of proscribing false science, lest any should be deceived by philosophy and vain deceit (Coloss. ii. 8).'— *Constitution on the Catholic Faith*, chap. iv. 'Of Faith and Reason.'

'I will not here attempt to enumerate the subject matters which fall within the limits of the Infallibility of the Church. It belongs to the Church alone to determine the limits of its own Infallibility. Hitherto it has not done so except by its acts, and from the practice of the Church we may infer to what matter its infallible discernment extends. It is enough for the present to show two things:—

'Firstly, that the Infallibility of the Church extends, as we have seen, directly to the whole matter of revealed truth, and indirectly to all truths which, though not revealed, are in such contact with revelation that the deposit of faith and morals cannot be guarded, expounded, and defended without an infallible discernment of such unrevealed truths.

'Secondly, that this extension of the Infallibility of the Church is, by the unanimous teaching of all theologians, at least theologically certain; and, in the judgment of the majority of theologians, certain by the certainty of faith.

'Such is the traditional doctrine respecting the Infallibility of the Church in faith and morals. By the definition of the Vatican Council, what is traditionally believed by all the faithful in respect to the Church is expressly declared of the Roman Pontiff. But the definition of the extent of that Infallibility, and of the certainty on which it rests, in matters not revealed, has not been treated as yet, but is left for the second part of the *Schema de Ecclesia*.

'Again, the definition declares the efficient cause of Infallibility to be a Divine assistance promised to Peter and in Peter to his successors.

'The explicit promise is that of our Divine Lord to Peter, "I have prayed for thee that thy faith fail not; and thou, being once converted, confirm thy brethren."[1]

'The implicit promise is in the words, "On this rock I will build my Church, and the gates of hell shall not prevail against it."[2] . . .

'The Divine assistance is therefore a *charisma*, a grace of the supernatural order, attached to the Primacy of Peter, which is perpetual in his successors.

'I need hardly point out that between the *charisma*, or *gratia gratis data*, of Infallibility and the idea of impeccability there is no connection. I should not so much as notice it, if some had not strangely obscured the subject by introducing this confusion. I should have thought that the gift of prophecy in Balaam and Caiaphas, to say nothing of the powers of the priesthood, which are the same in good and bad alike, would have been enough to make such confusion impossible.

'The preface to the Definition carefully lays down that Infallibility is not inspiration.

'The Divine assistance by which the Pontiff are guarded from error, when as Pontiffs they teach in matters of faith and morals, contains no new revelation. Inspiration contained, not only assistance in writing, but sometimes the suggestion of truths not otherwise known. The Pontiffs are witnesses, teachers, and judges of the revelation already given to the Church; and in guarding, expounding, and defending that reve-

---

[1] St. Luke xxii. 32.   [2] St. Matt. xvi. 18.

lation, their witness, teaching, and judgment are by Divine assistance preserved from error.'[1]

I will now answer Mr. Gladstone's question—why the Definition was made. The Vatican Council, then, defined the Infallibility of the Head of the Church, because, if it had failed to do so, the doctrinal authority of the Church would have been weakened throughout the world. Every motive of worldly policy would have tempted the Council to compromise, and to shrink from defining it; but the peremptory obligations of Divine Truth compelled it in defiance of all policy to define it. Necessity was laid upon the Council, and it could not recede. Universal doubt and scepticism are pervading men and nations: therefore the Church defined the Infallibility of its Head, which is the confirmation of its own. As a Divine witness, it declared his commission, and the powers given for its exercise. The Vicar of Jesus Christ testified to the world, wearied with doubt and sick with religious contentions, that the promise of his Master, 'He that heareth you heareth Me,' has not failed. The definition of the Infallible teaching of the Church by its Head affirms that there is still a divine certainty of faith upon earth; and that, as God is the sole Fountain of all Truth, so the Church is the only channel of its conveyance and custody among men. No other policy prompted the Definition. And even though the combined hostility of Civil Powers, as we now see it, had been heated sevenfold hot before its eyes, the Council would not have swerved from de-

---

[1] *Petri Privilegium*, part iii. pp. 56–60, 66, 78, 84. (Longmans 1870.)

claring, whether politic or not, the truth delivered to its charge. If I speak without hesitation, it is because I am able to speak of that which I saw with my own eyes, and heard with my own ears

I hope I shall not violate any confidence which ought to be sacred, or any reserve the delicacy of which I fully recognise, in going on to state a fact of which I am able to give personal testimony.

One day, during the deliberations of the Council, when the pressure of Diplomatists, and Governments, and journals was at its highest, the Holy Father said, 'I have just been warned that if the Council shall persist in making this definition, the protection of the French army will be withdrawn.' After a pause he added, with great calmness, 'As if the unworthy Vicar of Jesus Christ could be swayed by such motives as these.' I can with perfect certainty affirm that 'policy' had as little influence on the Council of the Vatican as it had on the Council of Nicæa; and that to ascribe the Definition to policy is as strange an aberration of judgment as to ascribe to the Definition the occupation of Rome, or the Franco-German war to thè Jesuits and to the Pope. When men say these things, can they believe them?

It needs but little of the historic spirit to perceive that if the Vatican Council, for such motives as these, ought to have abstained from defining the Infallibility of the Head of the Christian Church, the Council of Nicæa ought also to have abstained from defining the *Homöousion*. There was violence all round about it. There was the certainty of a schism. After the Council eighty Bishops apostatised. They appealed, as all heretics ever do, to the Civil Powers. The Arian Schism was formed; it was protected by Emperor after Emperor. Arianism became a State tool against the Catholic Church. It infected Constantinople; it spread into Italy and Spain; it lasted for centuries. But where is it now? And where now is the Creed of Nicæa? The *Homöousion* is at this day in the heart of the whole Church throughout the world. So will it be with the Council of the Vatican. What the Council of Florence implicitly declared, and the Council of Trent assumed as of faith, that the Council of the Vatican explicitly defined. It is very true that since the Council of Constance, that is, since the great schism of the West, when the Civil powers of Europe, for a time, shook the visible unity of the Church by endeavouring to lessen the authority of its Head, the power of the Roman Pontiff has steadily consolidated itself in the intellect and the will of the Church. What was believed from the beginning has been now forced into explicit declaration. But while the Church has thus been more and more defining its faith with a Divine precision, the world has wandered off farther and farther into the wilderness of unbelief. The Council of Trent defined the particular doctrines denied by Luther's Reformation. But it did not deal with the master principle on which it rested. The chief character of the sixteenth century was the denial of the Divine authority of the Church, secured to it in virtue of a perpetual assistance of the Spirit of Truth. Three hundred years have unfolded the consequences of this denial. It is nearly complete in the rationalism and infidelity of Germany. The 'Centuria prærogativa' has a mournful privilege of precedence in the Comitia of unbelievers. It has run its course, too, in Switzerland; and I must add, with sadness, it is running its course in the widespread doubt which is undermining the Christianity of England. Day after day I hear the words, 'I wish I knew what to believe, and why to believe anything:' and this from some of the noblest and most masculine natures, who recoil from the incoherence and contradiction of teachers who gainsay one another. But here is a subject on which I have no desire to enter. If I were asked to say what is the chief intellectual malady of England and of the world at this day, I should say, ubiquitous, universal doubt, an uncertainty which came in like a flood after the rejection of the Divine certainty of Faith. This uncertainty has already led multitudes to an entire rejection of Christianity; and they have not rested even in Deism. They have gone on to the rejection even of natural religion. They have no certainty that they have a conscience, or a will, or a soul, or a law of morality, or that there is a God. Three hundred years hence, when men look back upon the Council of the Vatican, as they now look back upon the Council of Trent—I will say even thirty years hence, when the noise and dust of the present conflict is laid,—they who have faith left in them will recognise the Divine guidance under which the Council of the Vatican declared the existence of God, with all the truths radiating from it, as resting upon the witness of the visible world; and also the Divine certainty of the Faith, as resting upon the witness of the Visible Church, and finding its perpetual and infallible expression in the voice of its Visible Head.

But it is now more than time to sum up what I hope has been sufficiently proved.

My first answer to the charge that the Vatican Council has made it impossible for Catholics to render a loyal civil allegiance, is that the Vatican Council has not touched our civil allegiance at all; that the laws which govern our civil allegiance are as old as the revelation of Christianity, and are regulated by the Divine constitution of the Church and the immutable duties of natural morality. We were bound by all these obligations before the Vatican Council existed. They are of Divine institution, and are beyond all change, being in themselves unchangeable. I have shown, I hope, that in the conflicts of the Civil Powers with the Church, the causes have arisen, not from acts of the Church, but from such acts as the Constitutions of Clarendon, the claim of Investitures, the creation of Royal Courts of final appeal, and the like; that these invasions of the Spiritual domain ever have been from the attempts of Governments to subject the Church to their own jurisdiction; and now more than ever, from an universal and simultaneous conspiracy against it. A leader of this conspiracy said the other day, 'The net is now drawn so close about the Church of Rome that if it escape this time I will believe it to be Divine.' If God grant him life, I have hope of his conversion. For, that the Church of Rome will escape out of the net is certain, and that for two reasons: first, for the same reason why its Divine Head rose again from the grave—'it was not possible that

He should be holden by it;'[1] and next, because the Civil Governments, that are now conspiring against it, are preparing for their own dissolution. Finally, I have given the true and evident reason why, when some six hundred Bishops from the ends of the Church were gathered together, they defined the Infallibility of their Head—'*Visum est Spiritui Sancto et nobis.*'

[1] Acts ii. 24.

CONCLUSION.

And now there only remains for me the hardest and saddest part of the task, which has not been sought by me, but has been forced upon me. A few months ago I could not have believed that I should have ever written these pages. I have never written any with more pain, and none of them have cost me so much as that which I am about to write.

Thus far I have endeavoured to confine myself to the subject-matter of Mr. Gladstone's pamphlet; but before I end, I feel bound by an imperative duty to lay before him, in behalf of his Catholic fellow-countrymen, the nature of the act which he has done.

He has not only invited, but instigated Catholics to rise against the Divine authority of the Catholic Church. He has endeavoured to create divisions among them. If Mr. Gladstone does not believe the authority of the Catholic Church to be Divine, he knows that they do.

If he thinks such a rising to be 'moral and mental freedom,' he knows that they believe it to be what his own Litany calls 'schism, heresy, and deadly sin.' If he believes religious separations to be lawful, he knows that they believe them to be violations of the Divine law. I am compelled therefore to say that this is at least an act of signal rashness.

No man has watched Mr. Gladstone's career as a statesman with a more generous and disinterested good-will than I have. No one has more gladly appreciated his gifts; no one has more equitably interpreted certain acts of his political life, nor has hailed his successes with greater joy. But when he casts off the character of a statesman, for which he has shown so great capacity, to play the Canonist and Theologian, for which he has here shown so little, and that with the intent of sowing discord and animosities among six millions of his fellow-countrymen—and, I must moreover add, with an indulgence of unchastened language rarely to be equalled—I feel bound to say that he has been betrayed into an act for which I can find no adequate excuse. I must tell him that if he would incline the Catholics of the Empire to accept the ministries of his compassion, he must first purify his style both of writing and of thinking. Catholics are not to be convinced or persuaded by such phrases as 'the present perilous Pontificate;' 'the Papal chair, its aiders and abettors;' 'the great hierarchic power and those who have egged it on;' 'the present degradation of the Episcopal order;' 'the subserviency or pliability of the Council;' 'hideous mummies;' 'head-quarters;' 'the follies of Ecclesiastical power;' 'foreign arrogance;' 'the myrmidons of the Apostolic Chamber;' 'the foreign influence of a caste.' I transcribe these words from his pages with repugnance; not, indeed, for our sake against whom they are levelled, but for the statesman who has thought them fitting. Mr. Gladstone can do many things; but he cannot do all things. He has a strong hand; but there is a bow which he cannot bend. He has here tried his hand at a task for which, without something more than mere literary knowledge, even his varied gifts will not suffice. This Expostulation is, as I have already said, an act out of all harmony and proportion with a great statesman's life.

I have written these words with a painful constraint; but, cost what it may, duty must be done, and I believe it to be my duty to record this judgment, in behalf of the Catholics of this country, on an act unjust in itself, and therefore not only barren of all good result, but charged with grave public dangers.

But, I cannot break off with a note so cheerless. If this Expostulation has cast down many hopes both of a public and a private kind, we cannot altogether regret its publication. If such mistrusts and misconceptions existed in the minds of our fellow-subjects the sooner and the more openly they were made public the better. We are not content to be tolerated as suspect or dangerous persons, or to be set at large upon good behaviour. We thank Mr. Gladstone for gaining us the hearing which we have had before the public justice of our country; and we are confident that his impeachment will be withdrawn. His own mind is too large, too just, and too upright to refuse to acknowledge an error, when he sees that he has been misled. It is also too clear and too accurate not to perceive that such is now the fact. I see in this the augury of a happier and more peaceful future than if this momentary conflict had never arisen. We shall all understand each other better. Our civil and religious peace at home will be firmer by this trial.

If the great German Empire shall only learn in time, thirteen millions of contented Catholic subjects, reconciled as they still may be by a return of just laws, will give a support to its unity which nothing can shake.

If Italy shall only come to see that the 'Roman question' is, and for ever will be, a source of weakness, contention, and danger to its welfare; and, seeing this, shall solve it peacefully, as Italy alone can do, by undoing its un-Catholic and therefore un-Italian policy, then its unity and independence will be secured by the spontaneous co-operation of a united people, gathered around the centre of all its Christian glories. Such a solution would then be consecrated by the highest sanctions of its faith. If wise counsels prevail, and wise friends of Italy shall gain its ear, it may be again what once it was, the foremost people in the Christian world.

And, lastly, for ourselves, our world-wide Empire cannot turn back upon its path without disintegration. It is bound together, not by material force, but by the moral bond of just laws and the glad consent of a free people. But justice and freedom cannot be put asunder. They flow from one source; they can be kept pure only by the same stream. They have come down to us from our Christianity. Divided as we are, we are a Christian people still. By religious conflict our Christianity will waste away as a moth fretting a garment. By religious peace, all that is true, and wise, and just, and Christian, will be perpetually multiplied, binding indissolubly in one all men and all races of our Imperial Commonwealth.

APPENDICES.

APPENDIX A.

INNOCENTIUS III. PRÆLATIS PER FRANCIAM CONSTITUTIS. A.D. 1200.

NOVIT Ille, qui nihil ignorat: *et infra.*

Non putet aliquis, quod jurisdictionem illustris Regis Francorum perturbare, aut minuere intendamus, cum ipse jurisdictionem nostram nec velit, nec debeat impedire. Sed cum Dominus dicat in Evangelio, 'Si peccaverit in te frater tuus, vade et corripe eum inter te et ipsum solum: si te audierit, lucratus eris fratrem tuum; si te non audierit, adhibe tecum unum vel duos, ut in ore duorum vel trium testium stet omne verbum. Quod si te non audierit, dic Ecclesiæ: si autem Ecclesiam non audierit, sit tibi sicut ethnicus et publicanus.'[1] Et Rex Angliæ sit paratus sufficienter ostendere, quod Rex Francorum peccat in ipsum, et ipse circa eum in correctione processit secundum regulam Evangelicam, et tandem quia nullo modo profecit, dixit Ecclesiæ. Quomodo nos, qui sumus ad regimen universalis Ecclesiæ superna dispositione vocati, mandatum divinum possumus non exaudire, ut non procedamus secundum formam ipsius? Nisi forsitan ipse coram nobis, vel Legato nostro, sufficientem in contrarium rationem ostendat. *Non enim intendimus judicare de feudo, cujus ad ipsum spectat judicium :* nisi forte jure communi per speciale privilegium, vel contrariam consuetudinem aliquid sit detractum: *sed decernere de peccato, cujus ad nos pertinet sine dubitatione censura, quam in quemlibet exercere possumus et debemus.* . . . . . Cum enim non humanæ constitutioni, sed divinæ potius innitamur, quia potestas nostra non est ex homine, sed ex Deo, nullus qui sit sanæ mentis ignorat, quin ad officium nostrum spectet de quocunque mortali peccato corripere quemlibet Christianum: et si correctionem contempserit, per districtionem ecclesiasticam coercere. Sed forsan dicetur,

[1] Matt. xviii. 15-17.

quod aliter cum regibus et aliter cum aliis est agendum. Cæterum scriptum novimus in lege divina: 'Ita magnum judicabis ut parvum; nec erit apud te acceptio personarum.'[1]—Corpus Juris Canonici, *Decret. Gregor.* lib. ii. tit. i. cap. xiii.

BONIFACIUS VIII., AD PERPETUAM REI MEMORIAM. A.D. 1302.

Unam Sanctam Ecclesiam Catholicam et ipsam Apostolicam urgente fide credere cogimur et tenere. Nosque hanc firmiter credimus et simpliciter confitemur: extra quam nec salus est, nec remissio peccatorum, Sponso in Canticis proclamante, 'Una est columba mea, perfecta mea: una est matri suæ, electa genitrici suæ:'[2] quæ unum corpus mysticum repræsentat, cujus caput Christus, Christi vero Deus. In qua unus Dominus, una fides, unum baptisma.[3] Una nempe fuit Diluvii tempore arca Noe, unam Ecclesiam præfigurans, quæ in uno cubito consummata,[4] unum, Noe videlicet, gubernatorem habuit et rectorem, extra quam omnis subsistentia super terram legimus fuisse deleta. Hanc autem veneramur et unicam; dicente Domino in Propheta, 'Erue a framea, Deus, animam meam et de manu canis unicam meam;'[5] pro anima enim, id est, pro seipso capite simul oravit et corpore: quod corpus unicam scilicet Ecclesiam nominavit, propter sponsi, fidei, sacramentorum et charitatis Ecclesiæ unitatem. Hæc est tunica illa Domini inconsutilis,[6] quæ scissa non fuit sed sorte provenit. Igitur Ecclesiæ unius et unicæ unum corpus, unum caput, non duo capita quasi monstrum, Christus videlicet, et Christi vicarius Petrus Petrique successor; dicente Domino ipsi Petro, 'Pasce oves meas,'[7] 'meas,' inquit, et generaliter non singulariter has vel illas, per quod commisisse sibi intelligitur universas. Sive ergo Græci, sive alii se dicant Petro ejusque successoribus non esse commissos, fateantur necesse se de ovibus Christi non esse; dicente Domino in Joanne 'unum ovile et unicum esse pastorem.'[8] In hac ejusque potestate duos esse gladios, spiritualem videlicet et temporalem, Evangelicis dictis instruimur. Nam dicentibus Apostolis, 'Ecce gladii duo hic,'[9] in Ecclesia scilicet, cum Apostoli loquerentur, non respondit Dominus nimis esse sed satis. Certe qui in potestate Petri temporalem gladium esse negat, male verbum attendit Domini proferentis, 'Converte gladium tuum in vaginam.'[10] Uterque ergo est in potestate Ecclesiæ, spiritualis

[1] Deut. i. 17.   [2] Cant. vi. 8.   [3] Eph. iv. 5.   [4] Gen. vi. 16.
[5] Psalm xxi. 21.   [6] Joann. xix. 23, 24.   [7] Joann. xxi. 17.
[8] Joann. x. 16.   [9] Luc. xxii. 38.   [10] Matt. xxvi. 52.

scilicet gladius et materialis. Sed is quidem pro Ecclesia, ille vero ab Ecclesia exercendus. Ille sacerdotis, is manu regum et militum, sed ad nutum et patientiam sacerdotis. Oportet autem gladium esse sub gladio et temporalem auctoritatem spirituali subjici potestati: nam cum dicat Apostolus, 'Non est potestas nisi a Deo, quæ autem sunt a Deo ordinata sunt:'[1] non autem ordinata essent, nisi gladius esset sub gladio, et tanquam inferior reduceretur per alium in suprema. Nam secundum beatum Dionysium, lex divinitatis est, infima per media in suprema reduci. Non ergo secundum ordinem universi omnia æque ac immediate, sed infima per media et inferiora per superiora ad ordinem reducuntur. Spiritualem autem et dignitate et nobilitate terrenam quamlibet præcellere potestatem, oportet tanto clarius nos fateri quanto spiritualia temporalia antecellunt. Quod etiam ex decimarum datione, et benedictione, et sanctificatione, ex ipsius potestatis acceptione, ex ipsarum rerum gubernatione claris oculis intuemur. Nam veritate testante, spiritualis potestas terrenam potestatem instituere habet et judicare, si bona non fuerit, sic de Ecclesia et ecclesiastica potestate verificatur vaticinium Hieremiæ: 'Ecce constitui te hodie super gentes et regna,'[2] et cætera quæ sequuntur. Ergo si deviat terrena potestas, judicabitur a potestate spirituali, sed si deviat spiritualis minor a suo superiori: si vero suprema, a solo Deo, non ab homine poterit judicari, testante Apostolo, 'Spiritualis homo judicat omnia, ipse autem a nemine judicatur.'[3] Est autem hæc auctoritas, etsi data sit homini et exerceatur per hominem, non humana, sed potius divina, ore divino Petro data, sibique suisque successoribus in ipso, quem confessus fuit petra firmata, dicente Domino ipsi Petro, 'Quodcunque ligaveris,'[4] etc. Quicunque igitur huic potestati a Deo sic ordinatæ resistit, Dei ordinationi resistit,[5] nisi duo sicut Manichæus fingat esse principia: quod falsum et hæreticum judicamus: quia testante Moyse, non in principiis, sed in principio cœlum Deus creavit et terram.[6] Porro subesse Romano Pontifici omni humanæ creaturæ declaramus, dicimus, definimus et pronunciamus omnino esse de necessitate salutis.

Datum Laterani xiv kal. Decembris, pontificatus nostri anno octavo.

Corpus Juris Canonici. *Extravag. Commun.* lib. i.
De Majoritate et Obedientia, cap. i.

CLEMENTIS V. DIPLOMA. A.D. 1306.

Clemens Episcopus, etc. Ad perpetuam rei memoriam.

Meruit carissimi filii nostri Philippi regis Francorum illustris sinceræ devotionis ad nos et Ecclesiam Romanam integritas, et progenitorum suorum præclara merita meruerunt meruit insuper fida regnicolarum pietas, ac devotionis sinceritas, ut tam regnum quam regem favore benevolo prosequamur. Hinc est quod nos dicto regi et regno per definitionem seu declarationem bonæ memoriæ Bonifacii PP. VIII. prædecessoris nostri, quæ incipit *Unam sanctam*, nullum volumus vel intendimus præjudicium generari. Nec quod per illam rex, regnum, regnicolæ prælibati amplius Ecclesiæ sint subjecti quam antea existebant. Sed omnia intelligantur in eodem esse statu quo erant ante definitionem præfatam, tam quantum ad Ecclesiam quam etiam quod regem et regnum superius nominatos.

Datum Lugduni kalendis Februarii, pontificatus nostri anno primo.

Labbe, *Concilia, sub ann.* 1305, tom. xiv. p. 1374,
ed. Ven. 1731.

APPENDIX B.

Extract from the Encyclical Letter of Gregory XVI. 'Mirari Vos,'
August 15, 1832.

As we have learned that certain writings spread abroad among the people publish doctrines which destroy the loyalty and submission due to princes, and kindle everywhere the torch of civil discord, we have to take especial care that the nations may not be deceived thereby, and led away from the right path. Let all bear in mind, according to the words of the Apostle, that 'there is no power but from God, and those that are ordained of God; therefore he that resisteth the power resisteth the ordinance of God, and they that resist purchase to themselves damnation.'[1]

Wherefore both divine and human laws cry out against those who, by basely plotting civil discord and sedition, abandon their allegiance to their princes and unite to drive them from their thrones.

[1] Rom. xiii. 2.

For this reason, to avoid so base a crime, it is a well-known fact that the first Christians, in the midst of persecutions, rendered meritorious service to their Emperors and to the safety of the Empire. This they showed by the clearest proofs, not only in fulfilling with all loyalty and promptitude all that was commanded them not contrary to their religion, but by persevering therein even to shedding their blood in battle for them.

'Christian soldiers,' says St. Augustine, 'served an unbelieving Emperor, but when the cause of Christ was in question, they acknowledged only Him who is in Heaven. They distinguished between the Eternal Lord and a temporal lord, and were nevertheless subject to the temporal for the sake of their Eternal Lord.'[1]

St. Maurice, the invincible martyr, the captain of the Theban Legion, had this before his eyes when, as St. Eucherius relates, he gave his answer to the Emperor:—' We are your soldiers, O Emperor, but nevertheless, we are free to confess, the servants of God. . . . And now we are not driven into rebellion, even to save our lives, for here we have arms in our hands, and we do not fight, because we have the will to die rather than to slay.'

This loyalty of the first Christians to their princes is the more conspicuous if we consider with Tertullian, that Christians at that time ' were not wanting in numbers and strength if they had wished for open war. We are but of yesterday, and we are found everywhere among you, in your cities, islands, strongholds, towns, public places, in your camps, your tribes, your companies, in your palaces, your senate, and your forum. . . . For what warfare should we not have been able and willing, even at great odds, who so readily offer ourselves to death, if our religion did not oblige us rather to die than to slay? . . . If we, so large a number as we are, had broken away from you and gone to some distant corner of the world, the loss of so many citizens, even such as we are, would have put your empire to shame, nay, would have punished you by the very loss. Without doubt you would have been daunted in your solitude. . . . You would have asked over whom you were ruling: more enemies would have been left than citizens: but now you have fewer enemies, owing to the number of Christians.'[2]

These luminous examples of immovable loyalty to princes, which necessarily followed from the holy precepts of the Christian religion,

[1] St. August. *in Psalm* cxxiv. n. 7.
[2] Tertullian *in Apolog.* cap. xxxvii.

at once condemn the detestable pride and wickedness of those who, boiling with unbridled lust for an inordinate liberty, are wholly engaged in destroying and tearing to pieces all the rights of princes in order to reduce the nations to slavery under pretence of liberty.—See *Recueil des Allocutions des Souverains Pontifes*. Paris, Le Clère, 1865, pp. 165-6.

APPENDIX C.

For the accuracy of the following statement I have direct evidence:

For several years past the Radical authorities of the Diocese of Basle have persecuted the Catholic Church, as they still continue to do. Formerly the persecution was carried into effect, partly by violence and partly by underhand means; but it was always specious and very injurious to religion. It was invariably carried on in the name of progress, liberty, and the welfare of the people, whom it pretended to free from the tyranny of the priesthood and the despotism of Rome.

The Catholic populations were thus oppressed by the so-called omnipotence of the State, and, incredible as it would seem under a republican form of government, the State, or rather a few individuals acting in its name, supported by a non-Catholic majority, and backed by the Radical element, have succeeded in monopolising power, and in maintaining themselves in it by terrorism and bribery for a length of years, assuming to themselves the functions of the Holy See and the Episcopate, and so adding to their temporal rule the spiritual government of souls. Not only have they possessed themselves of the direction of all public schools, and of the administration of all pious foundations, but they have destroyed all the monastic, capitular, and ecclesiastical institutions, claimed the right to regulate the parochial system, the preaching of the Gospel, catechising, confessions, first communions of children, the celebration of public worship, processions, burials and benedictions, and even extended their jurisdiction to matrimonial causes. More than this, by the Federal Constitution, which the recent revolutionary laws have just extended to the Catholic cantons, contrary to the will of the populations as expressed by the vote of an immense majority, the State has virtually and insidiously suppressed the Catholic Church by the introduction of that article of the Federal Code by which the ecclesiastical jurisdiction is abolished. (Art. 58.)

Finally, in five cantons of the Diocese of Basle, the Catholic populations have lost all liberty of worship in a more or less degree.

Since the Council of the Vatican more especially, the war against the Church has been waged with greater acrimony in the Diocese of Basle, and since the victories of Prussia, our enemies have acted more openly. The five governments of Soleure, Argovie, Basle-Campagne, Berne, and Thurgovie have sent their delegates to an assembly calling itself a Diocesan Conference, composed not of ecclesiastics, but in great part of Protestants, and of lay-Catholics notoriously hostile to the Church. Such a body of course possessed no legal authority, but notwithstanding its patent incapacity, it committed, among many other illegal and unjust acts, that of pronouncing a sentence of deprivation against the Bishop of Basle, on the 29th of January, 1873. The principal offence imputed to him was, that of having published the definition of Papal Infallibility in his diocese, and of having refused to withdraw the publication. Several minor accusations were brought against him; but it may be remarked that the authorities were unable to prove that he had violated a single law during the whole course of his episcopate. He was therefore deprived of his see solely because he had fulfilled the duties of a Catholic bishop, and because he would not separate himself from the Unity of the Holy See, by refusing to publish the decrees of the Vatican Council.

Since the above attack on the liberties of the Catholic populations, the Holy See, and the Church, a series of laws favouring schism and apostasy have been passed by the five cantonal governments in question. They have forbidden the Bishop of Basle to exercise his episcopal charge throughout the five cantons composing his diocese; and they have also forbidden the clergy to maintain any official relations with him, so that the faithful suffer grievous injury in their most sacred rights, and in their most urgent religious needs, in common with the whole Catholic priesthood, which has been punished in all the cantons for having protested against these unjust acts.

But it is the Protestant Canton of Berne which has signalised itself beyond all others by its despotism and its cruelty. It has suspended all the parish priests of the canton from their pastoral functions, and has since then deprived them, as well as all their curates, to the number of sixty-nine. It next pronounced sentence of exile on the whole clergy, ninety in number, only excepting five or six aged priests, who were, however, forbidden to say mass save in their own rooms, or in any way to exercise their sacred ministry. The government then drove all the priests out of their churches and presbyteries, and confiscated all their benefices and revenues, so that they are deprived of all means of subsistence. Before the sentence of exile was carried out, many of them were moreover punished by fine and imprisonment. The Catholic laity has suffered there, and still has to suffer from every kind of injustice: fines, imprisonment, dismissal from public employment, are common occurrences, and men, women, nuns, and even children have been imprisoned for their faith.

There are, at the present moment, more than 60,000 Catholics in the Canton of Berne, who are deprived, as far as State influence can effect it, of all religious help, whether in life or in death, the exiled priests of the Bernese Jura being arrested and cast into prison if discovered within the cantonal limits.

The immense majority of the people, however, remain firmly attached to their pastors. In many parishes not a schismatic is to be found, and in others, containing a numerous population, the exceptions are very few. In a word, the Catholics of the Bernese Jura maintain their fidelity to the faith of their fathers, and the only partisans of the schism are apostates or persons long notoriously hostile to the Church.

But the most revolting feature of the present persecution is that the Government of Berne has sought in every part of Europe foreign priests in order to replace the lawfully appointed clergy of the Jura. It has succeeded in finding a certain number of suspended or apostate priests, who have consented to act as the instruments of State persecution. During the fourteen months which have witnessed the exile of the sixty-nine faithful parish clergy, twenty-five strangers have been brought to replace them. These men are of the worst moral antecedents. The government, notwithstanding, has imposed them on the parishioners, gives them profuse supplies of money, makes over the churches and presbyteries to them, and supports them in every way, while the native clergy are despoiled and exiled.

The Catholics of the Jura being thus deprived of their pastors, meet in farms or outhouses for common worship; and yet even this liberty is not always conceded to them. It is only in profound secret they can receive the sacraments, or hear mass, and they even bury their own dead without the assistance of a priest. It is thus that religious animosity, making common cause with Radicalism, tyrannises over its fellow-citizens, who commit no offence against the public peace, and who bear their proportionate share of the public burdens!

By the course it has pursued the Government of Berne has violated the treaties and constitutions which protect Catholic liberties within the cantons. In order to give a colour of legality to future persecutions, it has voted a new Ecclesiastical Constitution, expressly framed against the interests of the Catholic Church in Switzerland, and which it has imposed, against their will, on the Catholics of Berne by a preponderant non-Catholic majority.

One consolation remains to us, namely, the fidelity of the entire body of clergy to the Catholic Church. They have freely chosen to lose all rather than betray the faith.

In order to perpetuate the supply of schismatic or 'Old-Catholic' priests, the government has recently established a faculty of theology in Berne. It has brought professors from Germany, either Protestants or apostate priests, and has induced a small number of students to follow the courses, by paying them highly for their attendance.

In Soleure, too, the Radical authorities carry on the same persecution of the Catholics of the cantons. The government has succeeded in placing three schismatical priests in as many parishes. It has suppressed and confiscated the celebrated and ancient abbey of the Benedictines at Mariastein and the Chapters of Schœnnenwerth and of the Bishopric of Basle at Soleure. In the other mixed cantons where the anti-Catholic Radicals are in a majority, the Catholics have much to suffer.

The Diocese of Basle includes seven cantons—viz. Soleure, Argovie, Thurgovie, Basle-Campagne, Berne, Lucerne, and Zug. The two last-named cantons are Catholic, and possess a just government. In the other cantons the majority is Protestant. To these must be added the city of Basle and the canton of Schaffhausen, both of which form part of the same diocese.

The Diocese of Basle comprises 430,000 Catholics and 800,000 Protestants and other denominations. It contains 800 priests, only seven of whom have become Old Catholics. The so-called Diocesan Conference has pushed its pretensions to the point of prescribing what authors are to be used by ecclesiastical students in the seminary! The bishop was not even free to appoint the superior and his assistants, but was obliged to obtain the 'Placet' of the State for such nominations, as well as for his Pastoral Letters.

www.ingramcontent.com/pod-product-compliance
Lightning Source LLC
Chambersburg PA
CBHW020251170426
43202CB00008B/328